7/26/2011

$ 11

D1061987

2011

Praise for
Trend Commandments

"Fire up the barbecue. Michael Covel skewers the sacred cows of Wall Street with tasty bite-sized bits of the truth about what it really takes to succeed in trading and life. Wide-ranging, irreverent, revealing, eminently quotable, and right on the money."

—**Charles Faulkner**, Market Wizard Trading Coach

"A rapidly moving, non-technical, and outside-the-box effort that smartly captures the essentials of trend following."

—**Peter Borish**, Chairman and CEO, Computer Trading Corp

"Covel's *Trend Commandments* offers a breezy rumination on what is *right* about trend following and what is *wrong* about conventional trading approaches."

—**Jack Schwager**, Author of *Market Wizards* and *Schwager on Futures* series

"Michael Covel's *Trend Commandments* is full of practical wisdom in bite-size portions on the benefits of trend trading—written in a straightforward storytelling format. It's definitely one to add to your financial bookshelf."

—**David Stendahl**, Signal Financial Group

"Michael Covel is the very best at explaining the concepts of successful trend following in plain English. I'm certain you'll be a successful trader if you follow the ideas he outlines in *Trend Commandments*. This book (and his previous two!) are required reading for new employees in my office."

—**Steve Sjuggerud**, DailyWealth

"An outstanding book for anyone who wants to become rich by trading markets. Today, government regulations and fiscal and monetary policies are badly distorting financial markets. Covel accurately explains why, in this 'manipulated' financial environment, you should never expect markets to move as you wish or expect. Rather, disregard your fundamental beliefs and simply follow the trend. Highly recommended!"

—**Marc Faber**, Managing Director, Marc Faber Ltd.,
and Editor, "Gloom Boom & Doom Report"

"Investors have experienced two bear markets in the last decade. This has led to rising volatility, uncertainty, and investor angst. For some it has been a lost decade, but for trend traders it has been a decade of opportunity. *Trend Commandments* helps you focus on what matters most: the trend of the markets, whether up or down. You can profit from either. *Trend Commandments* is essential reading for those who have the desire to thrive and survive in an era of fast-paced trending markets."

—**Jim Puplava**, CEO, Chief Investment Strategist, PFS Group

"Buy and hold has been a difficult investment system for investors for a decade. In *Trend Commandments*, Covel challenges readers to think differently and question their beliefs about market 'truths' ingrained in them for years. Forewarned, you just may never see the world the same way again."

—**Mebane Faber**, Cambria Investment Management

"If you are even thinking of a career in trading, put down all the other books. Buy this one. Read it. Now you can start your career."

—**James Altucher**, Managing Director, Formula Capital

TREND
COMMANDMENTS

TREND COMMANDMENTS

Trading for Exceptional Returns

Michael W. Covel

Vice President, Publisher: Tim Moore
Associate Publisher and Director of Marketing: Amy Neidlinger
Executive Editor: Jim Boyd
Editorial Assistant: Pamela Boland
Development Editor: Russ Hall
Senior Marketing Manager: Julie Phifer
Assistant Marketing Manager: Megan Colvin
Cover Designer: Chuti Prasertsith
Cover Design Idea: Michelle Sanks
Managing Editor: Kristy Hart
Project Editor: Betsy Harris
Copy Editor: Geneil Breeze
Proofreader: Sarah Kearns
Senior Indexer: Cheryl Lenser
Interior Designer: Gloria Schurick
Senior Compositor: Gloria Schurick
Manufacturing Buyer: Dan Uhrig

© 2011 by Michael W. Covel
Published by Pearson Education, Inc.
Publishing as FT Press
Upper Saddle River, New Jersey 07458

This book is sold with the understanding that neither the author nor the publisher is engaged in rendering legal, accounting, or other professional services or advice by publishing this book. Each individual situation is unique. Thus, if legal or financial advice or other expert assistance is required in a specific situation, the services of a competent professional should be sought to ensure that the situation has been evaluated carefully and appropriately. The author and the publisher disclaim any liability, loss, or risk resulting directly or indirectly, from the use or application of any of the contents of this book.

FT Press offers excellent discounts on this book when ordered in quantity for bulk purchases or special sales. For more information, please contact U.S. Corporate and Government Sales, 1-800-382-3419, corpsales@pearsontechgroup.com. For sales outside the U.S., please contact International Sales at international@pearson.com.

Company and product names mentioned herein are the trademarks or registered trademarks of their respective owners.

Printed in the United States of America

First Printing June 2011
ISBN-10: 0-13-269524-3
ISBN-13: 978-0-13-269524-4
Pearson Education LTD.
Pearson Education Australia PTY, Limited.
Pearson Education Singapore, Pte. Ltd.
Pearson Education North Asia, Ltd.
Pearson Education Canada, Ltd.
Pearson Educación de Mexico, S.A. de C.V.
Pearson Education—Japan
Pearson Education Malaysia, Pte. Ltd.
Library of Congress Cataloging-in-Publication Data
Covel, Michael.
    Trend commandments : trading for exceptional returns / Michael W. Covel. — 1st ed.
        p. cm.
    Includes bibliographical references.
    ISBN 978-0-13-269524-4 (hardcover : alk. paper)
    1. Investments. 2. Stocks. I. Title.
    HG4521.C818 2012
    332.63'22—dc22
                                                2011011412

To breakfast at Tiffany's...

This is your last chance. After this, there is no turning back. You take the blue pill—the story ends, you wake up in your bed and believe whatever you want to believe. You take the red pill—you stay in Wonderland and I show you how deep the rabbit hole goes.[1]

Contents

Acknowledgments

A very special thank you goes to Michelle Sanks, my editor and researcher in chief.

Also: Salem Abraham, James Altucher, Karla Anselmo, Greg Avallon, Arlana Aylward, Bryan Aylward, Bryan Bangerter, Aisha Barber, Jesse Barkasy, Steve Beamer, Marty Bergin, Peter Borish, Danielle Bourbeau, Tim Bourquin, Jim Boyd, Jason Burack, Gibbons Burke, Steve Burns, Sandy Brasher, Kevin Bruce, Jim Byers, Chuck Cain, Kavita Channe, Michael Clarke, CME, Jerome Covel, Johanna Covel, Mary Covel, Eric Crittenden, Luke David, Gary Davis, Rebecca Clear Dean, Gary DeMoss, Nikesh Desai, Bernard Drury, David Druz, Bill Dunn, Guy Edrington, Robin Eggar, Martin Ehrlich, David Eifrig, Billy Emerson, Alistair Evans, Mebane Faber, Charles Faulkner, Jack Forrest, Black Francis, Debbie Gallaher, Kevin Gallaher, William Gallwas, Danuza Gartner, Jason Gerlach, Marcus Gersbach, Michael Gibbons, Mark Gjormand, Dave Goodboy, Norman Hallett, David Harding, Esmond Harmsworth, Betsy Harris, Rika Heidemann, Betty Henon, Paul Henon, Larry Hite, Dalice Huffman, Ed Holiday, Brian Hurley, John Hurley, Patrick Hurley, Virginia Hurley, Withers Hurley, Brian Hunt, Bucky Isaacson, Marshall "Jake" Jacobs, Ajay Jani, Bobby Johns, JonPaul Jonkheer, Perry Jonkheer, Shaun Jordan, Chris Kacher, Joseph Kavaliauskas, Sylvester Kavaliauskas, Ken at Breakout Stocks, Jordan Kimmel, Martin Klitzner, Jeff Kopiwoda, David Kreinces, Krystal, Katrina Kurdy, Eric Laing, Kimberly Laube, Jeffrey Lay, Charles LeBeau, Jez Liberty, Lindsay LoBello, Sandy Lynn, Jeff Macke, Alex Mann, Erin Marie, Michael Martin, Paloma Martinez, Luci Mattinen, Brian McHugh, Mark Melin, Juan Carlos Mendoza, Todd Miller, Gareth Moore, Gil Morales, Jerry Mullins, Paul Mulvaney, Jered Murphy, Victor Niederhoffer, David Nott, Tom O'Connell, Matthew Osborne, Michelle Pelle, Julie Phifer, Tim Pickering, Jim Preston, Nancy Preston, Jim Puplava, Barry Ritholtz, Lloyd Ritter, Baron Robertson, Cullen Roche, Jim Rohrbach, Ian Rummer, Marlene Sanchez, Michelle Sanks, Barbara Schmidt-Bailey, Steve Segar, Ed Seykota, Greg Shaughnessy, Mike Shell, Marsha Shepard, Steve Sjuggerud, Richard Slaughter, Nell Sloane, Alex Spiroglou, David Stendahl, Clint Stevens, Matthew Stich, Susan Stich, Celia Straus, Leodalys Suarez, Jon Sundt, Timothy Sykes, Larry Tentarelli, Irve Towers, Dennis Tran, Francisco Vaca, Justin Vandergrift, Robyn Vandergrift, Trish Vianna, Damon Vickers, Danny Walsh, Matt Waz, Bryan Werlemann, Paul Wigdor, Addison Wiggin, Cole Wilcox, Bryce Woodall, Luciana Antonello Xavier, Daniele Yeonas, Monica Yeonas, Thai Yin, Jack Zaner, zerohedge.com.

Do not strive for things
occurring to occur
as you wish,
but wish the things
occurring as they occur,
and you will flow well.[1]

Ignition

Trading for exceptional returns may not appear realistic in the schizophrenic cacophony:

"What is the right approach for investors faced with an unusually uncertain economic outlook and volatile markets?"

"Big concerns over job insecurity, consumer and corporate spending, and housing prices."

"Should you buy gold?"

"Where are markets headed?"

"Oil shock, dollar drop, Japanese earthquake, elections!"

That's white noise.

Yes, sure, of course, you may have more options, but an explosion of naiveté has muddied the waters. Ignorance and confusion reign supreme. The idiot box is no longer just the bedroom flat screen. It is every PC, Mac, iPhone, and iPad. People absorb TMZ and Drudge via an intravenous drip. We are in a voyeuristic world where living vicariously through someone or something is accepted without hesitation and, in fact, encouraged.

With brain synapses bombarded nonstop, it is no surprise that this has brought attention spans down to just a few seconds—about the same as a goldfish. However, an incessant barrage of information across every known connected device will not punch your ticket to financial freedom.

Retirement plans that have elderly dining on cat food, buying gold because you are scared, canning food, and setting up a crisis garden are not solutions. If that's your direction, this book is a tough love punch to your gut. Brutal honesty about what it takes to get ahead with your money is coming in these pages like a hard rain. There is no reason to continue on the hamster wheel.

You simply need a winning philosophy and strategy, backed by proven positive results that you can execute. Push the pause button.

> You don't have to be a hamster running through a Habitrail®. "Despite all my rage I am still just a rat in a cage" is not fait accompli.[2]

In the film *Contact*, Jodie Foster plays a character called Ellie, a scientist who cannot figure out an alien signal from the deep reaches of outer space until she finds the key—the "primer." Finally she receives help from a Carl Sagan-like benefactor named S. R. Hadden:

> **Hadden:** The powers that be have been very busy lately, falling over each other to position themselves for the game of the millennium to decipher the alien signal. Maybe I can help deal you back in.
>
> **Ellie:** I didn't realize that I was out.
>
> **Hadden:** Oh, maybe not out, but certainly being handed your hat. I have had a long time to make enemies Doctor...and I wish to make a small contribution. A final gesture of goodwill to the people of this planet....
>
> **Ellie:** You've found the primer!
>
> **Hadden:** Clever girl.

Today, John W. Henry is the owner of the Boston Red Sox baseball team. He also now owns the famed Liverpool Football Club in Britain. Red Sox price: $700 million. Liverpool: $476 million. He is not broke.

How did he make that fortune?

Trading in a very rigid, rules-defined, way.

In 1995, Henry, a former farmer from Arkansas who began his trading career humbly hedging his crops, made speculative trading history. His trading strategies essentially *won* the money lost by rogue trader Nick Leeson of Barings Bank (often referred to as the "Queen's bank"). Leeson bet wildly and lost $1.3 billion. The Queen's bank collapsed. Leeson was the *Time* cover boy. Media ate up the bank's implosion and coverage was nonstop. Leeson was the known loser. Henry was the then-unknown winner.

Henry won practicing a form of trading called *systematic trend following*. His big win was never revealed (see my first book, *Trend Following*). Some tight insiders knew, but with detective-like probing, I outed Henry's win.

Just like S. R. Hadden, the primer to Henry's moneymaking system was deep in my mind *and* gut.

But money success is much more than some event in the long ago dotcom era. It is about an ongoing profit system that reaps spoils when markets crash and fear cascades—as in 2008. It's also about finding big trends to ride even when there is no panic or crisis. Trend following, however, is not theoretical or academic wonk talk. There are decades of substantial performance proof.

Big money making starts with trends, or waves. Anyone who makes significant money rides waves. And guess what? No one can predict the next big one. The only certainty is that when the big wave comes, trend followers will surf the new beaches.

That simple-sounding ideology is instrumental for financial flexibility, as trend followers trade that same philosophy in all markets. You can storm into any moving market, be it an obscure currency or a stock in wild emerging markets. Trend following is agnostic to both the market and direction. It is a James Bond "007 license" to pursue whatever market is flowing up or down.

Now, nearly 20 years after outsmarting the Queen's bank, John W. Henry and his trend trading peers still operate in an essentially secretive underground society, a financial parallel world. Henry's accomplishments are astounding, but many of his trend-trading peers have also killed it. Traders such as David Harding, Ken Tropin, Louis Bacon, and Bruce Kovner have become billionaires trading unpredictable trends.

Additionally, mysterious firms not built around individual names, are also making trend-chasing fortunes. Sunrise Capital, Transtrend, BlueCrest, Altis Partners, Aspect Capital, and Man Investments just to name a few, are some of today's top traders, pulling billions in profits out of the markets—quietly and effectively. While seemingly everyone else is mainlined into the *matrix* for a daily fix of mutual funds, news, and government, trend traders keep on keeping on. But this is not about hero worship; it's about *learning* from winners.

John W. Henry was recently asked how he did *that*—meaning make the money. He quipped, "I didn't do that. Mathematical formulas did that. It's made through trend following." The interviewer noted that the U.S. dollar was down and asked if he bet against it. Henry replied with a smile, "Right, very good." The interviewer said, "I don't get that." Henry with a touch of sarcasm added, "Neither will your readers."[3]

If you are thinking that I have inserted a conspiracy theory, *X-Files*, or Area 51 edge to trend following, smart thinking. Trend traders are dialed in and average investors are lost? Indeed. Many investors today hide their money under mattresses. Everything that used to be safe is now risky.

Real estate has cratered. Stocks are up one day, and down the next. Buy and *hope* with no S&P 500 Index returns for a decade. Dot-com bubble? Check, that disaster never left. Politicians on both sides of the aisle are just fear mongers. And let's not forget about salesmen hawking gold as a hedge against the end times.

Don't fret! There is good news. This book is real hope. It is the *primer* that unlocks the path of trend trading.

Trend Commandments is a new inspirational vantage. It is not my prior books. The tone is different. The style is different. Its objective is to be more accessible and rooted in principles over personalities. I thought a different approach to get this story out was required, for very few are yet aware of what's in these pages.

> If you are not criticized, you might not be doing much.

Sadly, many still see making money wrong. They make wildly inaccurate assumptions about what constitutes a winning trader:

- Do they possess a unique talent?
- A special inborn gene or divine gift?
- The innate talent of a child prodigy?
- Inside knowledge?
- Ability to predict markets?
- Degrees in finance or an MBA?
- Huge starting capital?

One answer: No.

Why do we not know that? Instant gratification is our Achilles' heel. Multitask this and that. Kardashians. Now. Faster. Easier. Patience is a four-letter word.

How does the latest iPad help you to make money trading the markets? How does attending a Code Pink or Tea Party rally help? How does connected 24/7 help you? TweetDeck, favorite blog, fancy broker tools…all will do what? How does electing your favorite politician help you to make money? How would changing the government in Egypt, Libya, or the United States for that matter make your retirement easier?

> Tomorrow is always another day in the dream factory.

Let's be honest. It's all about you. It's you, your friends, and your family against the world. This book is for people who want above and beyond an average. It's about getting wealthy and thriving. Now, faster, and easier doesn't work for market prosperity. That's not strategy. Trend following traders don't play that way, and neither should you.

Ten years ago, Jason Fried of 37signals.com was hired as my first pro web site designer. He has since moved on to ventures far exceeding simple web site design, so it was very random that his book *Rework* inspired me to write *Trend Commandments*. His big question made me think:

"Taking a stand always stands out. Who do you want to take a shot at?"[4]

A valid question. My answer: Wall Street, the government, and media for starters.

Let go of them.

That is a breath of fresh air in an era of constant depression and recession talk, nonstop predictions, clueless economists, and Federal Reserve Ponzi schemes. *Trend Commandments* is for those who know deep down that there is a real way to make money in the markets, but just do not know how yet.

However, you will be surprised that the *secret* is hiding in plain sight.

There was a great story on author Seth Godin's web site. He had a college professor who worked as an engineering consultant. There was a 40-story office tower in Boston with a serious problem—an unsightly dark smudge was coming through the drywall. The multimillion-dollar fix would be to rip out all the drywall. Godin's former professor was hired in a last-ditch effort. He said, "I think I can fix it, but it will cost you $45,000." The owners instantly agreed. The professor wrote down the name of a common hardware store chemical. "Here," he said and sent a $45,000 bill. It was a bargain.[5]

The words condensed into *Trend Commandments* were gleaned from my 15 years of behind-the-scenes learning at the feet of great trend following traders. It was a one-of-a-kind educational journey. My books *Trend Following* and *The Complete TurtleTrader* have sold more than 100,000 copies (no bragging, just for reference). My documentary film *Broke* outlined the Great Recession from a trend following perspective. That took three years and 100,000 travel miles alone.

> Trend following starts with knowing when to do nothing. The market is screaming like a spoiled brat? Step to the side. That's your first play.

You might argue against my words, but arguing against my passion and research will be exhausting. Trust me, but verify every word herein. Accept nothing without questioning why. Find holes in the arguments, and when you can't, send me a thank you card.

You want confidence and inspiration? It's here.

Note: There are not only 10 trend commandments. There are dozens of perspectives, comparisons, critiques, rules, and examples herein. And don't feel compelled to read linearly; start anywhere. Also, be careful that you don't singularly fixate on trading rules alone (read: entry/exit). If you exclude the discipline, psychology, and perseverance, etc., needed to excel in the long run, you won't make it.

*If you must play, decide upon
three things at the start:
the rules of the game,
the stakes,
and quitting time.*[1]

Expectations

Who will *Trend Commandments* reach?

This book is for those kindred spirits who grasp there is no secret to trading but rather just knowledge you have not yet discovered. It is for anyone who wants to make the most money possible—without going broke or going overboard on risk.

It is for investors and traders small and large, young and old, female and male—worldwide. *Trend Commandments* is also for anyone fascinated by how great trend traders think and act to make a fortune. If you have other reasons for reading this book, that is fine too.

> Panics do not destroy capital—they merely reveal the extent to which it has previously been destroyed by its betrayal in hopelessly unproductive works.[2]

My words are not a set of magic rules for becoming a wealthy trend following trader with no work on your end. To achieve the pot of gold, you will need more than *that*. However, to explain all the details you will need, you must know what you are up against.

The well-constructed fortress of government, media, and Wall Street, all designed to bleed you dry, is "The Wall" (think Roger Waters). None of those players want you to comprehend or act on the contents of this book. If you do get it, those groups lose power and money. They do not want to lose anything. Their grip on you is stranglehold tight.

> There cannot be a suggestion that the attempt of describing, explaining, predicting, and controlling is wrong, no matter how foolish it may appear. Let men be fools because that is part of their nature.[3]

Getting rich is a fight; make no mistake about it.

Henry Ford: "If I'd asked my customers what they wanted, they would have said a faster horse."[1]

Jargon

To avoid confusion throughout *Trend Commandments*, a few of Wall Street's favorite catch phrases need to be defined. I am defining these because Wall Street suits use them to *sell*. Do not let the jargon engulf you.

CTA: CTA stands for commodity trading advisor. It is a government term used to classify regulated fund managers who primarily trade futures markets. Almost all successful CTAs trade as trend following traders. CTAs are the other quants the media never seems to cover accurately.

Managed Futures: This is a term that describes regulated fund managers who use futures to trade for clients. It is an awful term because it fixates on the instrument (futures), not the strategy. Here's the dirty little secret: Almost all successful managed futures trading firms use a trend following strategy. The term is often used interchangeably with CTA. Noted radio host and author Dave Ramsey recently had this to say about managed futures:

> "The term *managed futures* is virtually an oxymoron...with managed futures you're basically betting on the future price of a commodity. What's the price of gold, or oil, or wheat going to be somewhere down the road? You're guessing as to what the future will bring, and managing a group of those guesses. What a joke!"[2]

If after reading *Trend Commandments* you share Dave Ramsey's view and understanding, I recommend a full frontal lobotomy as your best wealth-building plan.

High Frequency Trading: High frequency trading is the latest term to describe arbitrage— at whatever time frame. It is about getting an advantage through speed and access. Most people are not going to enter the world of high frequency trading (or be Goldman Sachs). It's a nonissue for your trading success.

> Whenever there is market movement, it is necessary for a Wall Street analyst to feel that he or she knows why it occurred. Almost always what they say is worthless.

Global Macro or Systematic Global Macro: Global macro is another term used to describe trend following traders, but indirectly. They do not say managed futures, and they do not say hedge fund, so it is global macro. It might make wealthy investors in Liechtenstein and Saudi Arabia feel more secure. The strategy is still trend following.

Hedge Fund: Think unregulated mutual fund that can trade in all markets up and down. Most hedge funds have terrible strategy: They are *long only* on leveraged stocks. That's it. Not as sexy as the press makes it. Of course, it all depends, and some hedge funds do make a killing. Usually, they are of the systematic trend following variety.

Long Only: Long only means you make one bet. You bet that the market will always go up.

Buy and Hold: Buy and hold (hope) is the same as long only.

Index Investing: You buy the S&P 500 Index and whatever it does is the return you get.

Value Investing: Attempts to use fundamentals to uncover *undervalued* stocks. The belief is you are buying cheap or low (terms that can mean anything to anyone). When that doesn't work out, you call the government and ask for a bailout.

Quant: You use formulas and rules, not daily discretion or fundamentals to make trading decisions. That said, unless quant is defined with precision you can never know what it means exactly. Trend following is a form of quant trading.

Repeatable Alpha: Alpha is return generated from trading skill. If you buy and hold the S&P 500 Index, and if it makes a positive return, that's not alpha. That return is beta for there was no skill involved. Repeatable alpha is simply the nice academic way of saying profit from skill. Trend following's argument as the only repeatable alpha is tough to counter.

Beta: The return you get for accepting the average. There is no skill involved. Think about a monkey aimlessly throwing darts against the wall— it's that level of skill.

Long: You buy a stock or futures contract.

Short (verb): The ability to profit from a decline in price of a stock or futures contract.

S&P 500: Is widely regarded as the best single gauge of large cap U.S. equities. The index was first published in 1957 and includes 500 leading companies.

Moving Average: A moving average series can be calculated for any time series, but is most often applied to market prices. Moving averages are used to smooth out short-term fluctuations, thus highlighting potentially longer-term trends.

A Vulcan mind-meld allows the sharing of thoughts, experiences, memories, and knowledge with another individual—via touch.

Average True Range: http://en.wikipedia.org/wiki/Average_True_Range (look this one up if you don't know it!).

There's no earthly way of knowing,
Which direction we are going,
There's no knowing where we're rowing,
Or which way the rivers flowing,
Is it raining?
Is it snowing?
Is a hurricane a-blowing?
Not a speck of light is showing,
So the danger must be growing,
Are the fires of hell a-glowing?
Is the grisly reaper mowing?
Yes, the danger must be growing,
Cause the rowers keep on rowing,
And they're certainly not showing,
Any signs that they are slowing![1]

Show Me the Money

Some say, "There's no romance in trend following." It's a matter of perspective. The romance is found in returns. Money…the ultimate aphrodisiac.

Performance data examples that follow could be the foundation of *every* college finance class. When you show up on the first day, instead of your teacher handing you a syllabus and telling you to buy certain books, you are handed one piece of paper that simply shows the performance histories of professional trend following traders for the last 50 years.

The entire semester could be built around *that* study alone. But first, to judge systematic trend following performance, you need a baseline. The S&P 500 is the barometer for making money in the markets. Comparing to it is wholly appropriate (even though some might carp).

Who are some of the top-performing trend following traders over the last 30 years? How much have they made? Consider the wealth generation:

- Bruce Kovner is worth more than $4.1 billion.[2]
- John W. Henry is worth $840 million.[3]
- Bill Dunn made $80 million in 2008.[4]
- Michael Marcus turned an initial $30,000 into $80 million.[5]
- David Harding is now worth more than $690 million.[6]
- Ed Seykota turned $5,000 into $15 million over 12 years.[7]
- Kenneth Tropin made $120 million in 2008.[8]
- Larry Hite has made millions upon millions over 30 years.[9]
- Louis Bacon is worth $1.7 billion.[10]
- Paul Tudor Jones is worth $3 billion.[11]
- Transtrend, a trend-trading fund, has produced hundreds of millions, if not billions, in profit.
- Trend following trader Man Group trades $68.6 billion in assets.[12]

From January 1980 to December 2008, the Barclays CTA Index achieved a 2805 percent return, or a 12.2 percent compounded average annual return. The Barclay CTA Index is a representative performance index of trend traders. For 2010, there were 533 traders included in the index.

> Neither assets under
> management,
> nor fortune made,
> tell you how good a trend
> trader is, but
> they do establish
> serious credibility.

Some miss the point:

"You are just touting super successful traders. What does that have to do with me?"

These names are featured for one reason: Proof.

Their returns are a precise illustration of what can be earned via trend following trading. Consider this nearly 40-year track record of trend trading wealth building:

Chart 1: Bill Dunn

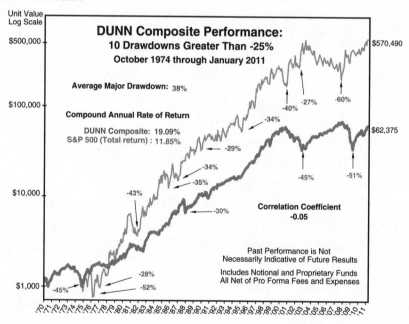

That picture is worth a thousand words. He is not alone.

Chart 2: Mark J. Walsh (Second-Generation TurtleTrader)—Monthly Returns

	Jan	Feb	Mar	Apr	May	Jun	Jul	Aug	Sep	Oct	Nov	Dec	YTD
2010	-2.49%	-4.27%	-1.29%	-2.11%	11.06%	2.73%	2.38%	4.92%	10.76%	10.08%	-4.86%	9.11%	39.91%
2009	-5.07%	-3.35%	-0.78%	-1.81%	8.87%	-4.27%	-1.24%	-1.25%	-1.85%	-8.28%	6.42%	-8.04%	-19.97%
2008	13.86%	19.55%	-10.03%	5.85%	3.98%	6.95%	-8.97%	3.44%	-1.71%	7.62%	2.27%	2.35%	50.30%
2007	2.42%	2.36%	-4.42%	4.27%	-1.42%	3.39%	-0.50%	-2.54%	11.30%	-5.08%	5.38%	3.66%	19.17%
2006	-1.93%	-5.84%	4.43%	23.68%	-2.26%	-10.21%	-6.76%	0.66%	-3.96%	2.72%	9.85%	-10.93%	-5.17%
2005	-8.13%	6.73%	-3.61%	-4.27%	3.98%	0.09%	-4.63%	5.77%	1.73%	-3.91%	7.26%	-3.10%	-3.50%
2004	5.85%	8.19%	4.09%	-6.87%	-0.41%	-5.33%	3.20%	-0.47%	2.12%	4.85%	8.81%	-4.70%	19.37%
2003	5.66%	4.35%	-12.40%	1.77%	9.74%	-4.18%	-0.06%	0.40%	7.12%	1.79%	-4.94%	3.56%	11.32%
2002	-6.57%	-3.63%	3.16%	-3.49%	10.10%	16.98%	12.46%	1.42%	8.19%	-9.70%	-2.89%	17.23%	46.46%
2001	0.88%	-3.67%	12.14%	-8.69%	-4.52%	-3.24%	-0.09%	7.19%	7.06%	3.76%	-9.61%	-3.78%	-4.88%
2000	0.92%	-3.34%	1.83%	1.12%	5.23%	2.56%	-2.19%	5.03%	-4.66%	-0.34%	6.10%	22.84%	37.92%
1999	-2.96%	16.10%	-7.88%	0.88%	-2.25%	-1.75%	0.87%	-8.04%	7.03%	-16.21%	1.80%	-3.01%	-17.39%
1998	5.61%	4.64%	-7.14%	-11.09%	2.82%	3.43%	-2.73%	40.83%	12.85%	-1.81%	0.58%	-5.33%	40.24%

Chart 3: David Druz—Monthly Returns

	Jan	Feb	Mar	Apr	May	Jun	Jul	Aug	Sep	Oct	Nov	Dec	Annual
2010	-1.63	-3.23	4.88	2.26	-2.40	3.24	-0.54	-3.65	19.98	18.27	9.23	10.55	68.90
2009	0.30	-1.12	-8.39	-2.65	15.67	-3.40	5.33	10.29	-1.99	-1.49	10.46	-1.98	20.00
2008	8.09	21.39	-7.18	0.14	2.05	6.78	-12.30	-1.64	-1.15	26.62	1.38	1.98	48.35
2007	-6.33	-1.68	-7.15	8.58	-0.61	6.76	-1.66	-10.49	26.03	3.69	-7.52	1.91	6.84
2006	16.31	-6.10	6.94	15.83	1.00	-2.61	-10.06	4.52	-4.15	-0.28	8.02	-3.79	24.26
2005	-4.20	1.12	-3.78	-3.03	4.16	-0.47	-3.80	6.90	0.71	-4.01	9.14	5.22	6.98
2004	4.51	14.38	1.44	-18.94	-7.83	-7.31	6.49	-3.17	5.98	4.00	12.75	0.39	8.04
2003	10.47	9.08	-7.41	4.31	6.11	-6.42	-7.00	0.34	1.71	12.69	-2.04	6.75	29.26
2002	-5.52	0.90	-0.43	-3.55	9.82	9.78	3.65	4.48	3.59	-3.01	2.27	9.58	34.58
2001	-1.79	2.46	13.89	-7.74	3.04	3.61	-3.37	1.99	5.29	8.13	-9.62	1.55	16.26
2000	3.82	-0.18	-4.05	1.34	8.37	-3.59	-1.20	3.46	-1.01	4.57	9.67	8.64	32.74
1999	-12.38	1.98	-8.81	4.56	-9.82	-1.91	0.93	2.77	5.24	-14.95	2.85	3.21	-25.74
1998	-1.63	-4.06	-2.24	-4.47	3.80	5.11	-0.97	18.34	-1.82	-1.94	-6.00	11.03	13.23
1997	10.50	9.17	-1.09	-5.72	8.00	-11.57	14.29	4.03	4.68	-2.06	0.08	5.10	37.75
1996	-8.81	-4.21	4.85	32.24	-7.49	2.68	-8.39	4.68	9.63	10.13	9.17	-6.43	36.07
1995	-7.78	2.33	16.84	6.61	12.27	2.46	-8.18	-5.91	-3.06	2.17	6.47	34.82	66.06
1994	-14.33	-14.53	-0.68	0.16	10.39	0.82	-5.71	-8.34	4.15	3.82	16.43	2.94	-9.20
1993	0.87	15.21	-7.68	-0.10	6.00	6.20	17.40	5.75	-6.69	-4.53	5.75	4.93	48.08
1992	-6.55	-10.29	-1.80	12.15	-2.29	17.82	17.05	7.17	-0.22	-5.10	2.98	-6.34	21.78
1991	-19.09	-4.71	4.69	-6.51	-5.08	8.29	-5.96	-10.11	4.25	2.62	-1.95	27.58	-12.26
1990	6.01	7.62	7.67	9.56	-9.23	5.49	16.26	10.78	18.20	3.52	1.29	-4.49	96.46
1989	1.30	-9.37	3.74	-10.69	20.27	-11.22	3.85	-11.94	-1.46	-26.02	3.81	11.39	-29.98
1988	-4.58	4.97	-11.75	-21.37	22.55	71.56	-10.03	3.71	1.50	-3.14	5.68	5.06	48.83
1987	-0.65	-5.08	-0.72	63.28	9.50	-6.93	10.98	-10.46	0.75	-13.38	13.89	12.05	72.39
1986	1.93	33.74	0.23	-11.98	-4.52	-15.24	4.03	2.49	-19.08	-19.45	-6.30	8.19	-31.43
1985	-1.39	-2.95	1.10	-1.44	-1.81	-7.37	28.33	2.76	-11.68	14.37	-0.81	-6.61	7.03
1984	-3.47	-8.69	-0.79	-4.05	12.41	-1.71	16.59	-4.68	2.62	-4.94	-3.87	3.81	0.30
1983	5.13	2.06	-6.92	-0.84	18.65	-18.61	6.02	30.98	-7.11	5.73	-11.36	3.23	19.34
1982	7.51	4.74	7.36	-0.34	1.47	5.74	-3.73	17.39	14.70	-8.39	-4.44	-11.16	30.32
1981							-2.63	8.22	-2.06	-4.20	15.00	2.42	16.46

Chart 4: Altis Partners—Monthly Returns

Year	Jan	Feb	Mar	Apr	May	Jun	Jul	Aug	Sep	Oct	Nov	Dec	YTD
2010	-2.50%	1.19%	4.93%	0.45%	-4.37%	-3.69%	0.01%	6.69%	2.94%	4.18%	-3.69%	5.62%	11.48%
2009	-3.21%	0.18%	-2.38%	-1.64%	2.47%	-3.23%	-0.31%	1.84%	2.13%	-5.22%	3.86%	-2.86%	-8.48%
2008	-4.31%	22.21%	-7.22%	-1.81%	10.57%	13.99%	-17.45%	-7.43%	9.05%	23.22%	3.74%	6.22%	51.91%
2007	2.13%	-3.91%	-4.58%	7.02%	3.10%	9.43%	-5.78%	-5.23%	8.71%	9.19%	-4.06%	4.21%	19.85%
2006	7.51%	-5.67%	7.16%	13.12%	0.37%	-4.75%	-5.49%	4.64%	0.69%	2.17%	3.56%	4.08%	28.90%
2005	-2.39%	-4.41%	3.27%	-3.56%	0.47%	2.31%	4.79%	4.79%	13.02%	-4.52%	14.03%	-0.81%	28.02%
2004	6.19%	14.55%	-0.10%	-11.03%	-5.25%	-4.22%	2.03%	-5.36%	2.72%	2.77%	-1.41%	0.00%	-1.38%
2003	10.12%	7.80%	-9.51%	5.35%	5.77%	-3.31%	-5.83%	-3.92%	-1.44%	13.07%	1.04%	6.45%	25.52%
2002	-3.18%	0.18%	-6.31%	3.54%	1.87%	7.64%	3.65%	5.21%	10.50%	-4.47%	2.42%	8.11%	31.49%
2001							-0.01%	2.70%	6.02%	5.78%	-6.25%	0.30%	8.29%

Chart 5: Howard Seidler (TurtleTrader)—Monthly Returns

Year	Jan	Feb	Mar	Apr	May	Jun	Jul	Aug	Sep	Oct	Nov	Dec	YTD
2010	-1.66	0.96	1.96	2.86	-5.91	0.04	0.52	0.79	6.27	5.11	-1.72	2.23	11.44
2009	1.07	0.22	-0.79	0.33	5.68	-0.59	2.18	4.34	3.06	-0.54	4.02	-0.33	20.01
2008	8.24	18.33	0.28	1.09	3.94	2.78	-4.87	-2.12	-0.84	2.09	3.77	0.33	36.12
2007	-4.35	2.84	-2.87	-1.41	0.08	5.15	6.13	-10.73	15.84	8.34	9.06	7.78	38.54
2006	7.79	0.67	-0.54	15.27	3.79	-3.31	-5.14	-1.54	0.68	-2.67	6.94	-10.15	9.79
2005	-5.93	-1.69	3.85	-9.55	6.54	-3.67	-8.97	-2.89	-2.21	1.47	6.05	7.54	-10.81
2004	3.13	8.56	4.44	-10.36	0.06	-6.29	-5.93	0.63	4.11	-0.77	10.99	-1.80	4.76
2003	15.21	3.87	-11.59	8.85	19.11	-3.69	1.43	1.20	12.04	21.16	-8.70	12.34	88.81
2002	-4.32	-8.51	7.89	-15.01	14.39	16.58	10.60	1.50	12.61	-9.14	-20.54	11.89	9.31
2001	-3.61	-1.52	-2.87	-3.20	-0.42	4.91	8.71	-2.68	1.29	19.21	-11.17	8.11	14.39
2000	-0.26	8.01	0.68	-7.50	7.09	2.50	1.67	3.34	-1.24	-10.38	16.45	17.55	40.18
1999	4.35	-1.37	-3.48	9.50	-16.15	3.96	-0.92	23.01	7.23	-5.87	5.91	0.80	24.53
1998	1.30	-4.55	-3.27	-7.84	-0.05	-6.06	0.77	47.13	12.24	2.19	-5.56	-2.82	26.31
1997	6.83	19.29	12.09	-8.24	-7.10	4.23	10.49	-23.15	19.32	-16.04	-4.69	3.56	6.56
1996	-5.59	-13.44	-21.65	44.99	-30.54	11.65	-0.40	0.97	30.63	37.01	10.66	-17.53	18.26
1995	-25.79	-8.54	38.90	7.36	-13.59	3.70	-34.45	-19.52	-6.98	-4.91	6.80	19.39	-46.04
1994	-16.98	-22.70	11.59	-17.90	41.14	37.85	17.52	-11.67	13.99	22.30	15.43	26.96	142.60
1993											9.47	27.47	39.54

Chart 6: Tom Shanks (TurtleTrader)—Monthly Returns

Year	Jan	Feb	Mar	Apr	May	Jun	Jul	Aug	Sep	Oct	Nov	Dec	YTD
2010	1.08	4.31	-1.25	6.87	0.73	4.53	5.68	6.52	8.94	5.17	-6.70	11.79	57.61
2009	-0.53	-3.08	-9.51	-13.63	15.69	-6.58	-2.83	1.35	5.50	-3.17	20.91	-14.50	-15.31
2008	23.53	11.12	0.20	0.32	4.57	-5.19	-6.98	19.38	6.28	15.46	-0.61	6.03	96.45
2007	-1.72	-6.77	-7.26	2.74	2.77	2.05	11.78	-2.62	25.62	-11.73	4.85	3.98	20.48
2006	2.04	-15.11	-3.63	26.13	-1.36	-1.99	-11.36	2.14	-9.35	-1.43	21.15		-0.24
2005	-8.83	15.63	-2.09	-10.20	7.11	0.79	-2.06	4.91	-8.57	-4.92	1.40	11.67	1.21
2004	1.30	6.15	-0.87	-8.66	-2.01	-5.86	-4.39	3.95	-3.28	1.48	8.20	-3.86	-8.86
2003	3.52	5.48	-15.81	5.05	17.28	4.28	1.52	2.06	4.34	-1.19	-8.54	10.57	27.59
2002	-4.97	-13.18	17.07	-8.14	9.06	15.04	17.03	3.45	4.78	-7.95	-4.47	9.82	36.37
2001	2.91	-3.53	2.25	-16.21	-0.11	0.14	11.41	15.06	10.39	11.09	-7.12	-1.18	22.76
2000	4.71	-1.46	-4.68	-9.80	5.11	-4.80	-13.50	14.61	-8.51	-3.43	15.01	39.51	24.76
1999	-3.47	7.25	4.74	1.56	-5.55	6.11	-7.05	-8.89	-6.54	-15.41	7.26	-4.81	-24.55
1998	14.31	-0.84	-6.65	-19.50	-1.66	-3.86	-6.24	80.29	5.48	-8.16	0.92	7.99	43.72
1997	10.73	10.71	13.78	-10.38	6.86	-1.47	26.07	-16.63	6.84	1.30	0.95	14.80	73.51
1996	-2.80	-7.30	-13.60	10.40	-9.10	-3.30	-8.89	-5.20	8.10	27.70	9.10	-26.30	-27.57
1995	-28.65	2.14	11.08	-4.42	8.78	-2.38	-11.32	14.48	-2.63	-8.72	0.76	23.34	-7.86
1994	-17.64	0.63	19.56	-6.11	17.96	24.00	-7.12	-16.63	22.37	-17.58	21.50	-13.67	11.48
1993	3.03	11.01	4.24	30.97	4.87	10.80	15.30	5.42	-6.13	2.65	-5.96	7.22	114.26
1992	-22.18	-13.61	6.67	-6.82	-2.91	18.10	11.18	13.20	20.40	5.90	2.08	-6.59	17.24
1991	-40.07	-7.14	13.52	-12.86	-9.17	12.43	-14.19	-9.18	9.69	-5.87	0.42	54.28	-29.92
1990	0.90	19.65	12.83	30.52	-10.10	11.64	34.75	21.87	37.93	-1.23	-5.54	-6.49	252.61
1989	-19.40	-14.20	20.26	-8.01	51.65	3.69	-10.28	-21.02	0.06	-20.06	33.40	73.30	57.63
1988											-7.40	21.00	12.05

Chart 7: Sunrise Capital: Most Profitable Trades 2008–2010

2008	2009	2010
Heating Oil – long	Copper – long	Cotton – long
Pound/Swiss Franc – short	Gold – long	Gold – long
Cotton – short	NASDAQ Index – long	Coffee – long
S&P500 Index – short	Zinc – long	Singapore $ – long
Crude Oil – long	Australian $ – long	Gold – long
Nickel – short	Sugar – long	Silver – long
Euro/Pound – long	S&P Index – long	Soy Meal – long
Nikkei Trade 1 – short	Gasoline (Rbob) – long	South African Rand – long
Nikkei Trade 2 – short	NZ$ – long	Soy Beans – long
Copper – short	Crude Oil – long	Japanese Yen – long
Euro Stoxx – short	Euro Stoxx – long	Zinc – long
Crude Oil – short[13]	Brent Oil – long[14]	Copper – long[15]

> Many trend followers do not achieve the highest returns possible, as they are often focused on accommodating clients who can't stomach what is required to achieve the big returns.

Paul Mulvaney (Mulvaney Capital) is a trend following trader too. Here are his last five years of trend following performance:

2010: +34.90%

2009: –5.89%

2008: +108.87%

2007: –23.14%

2006: +21.94%[16]

Big numbers like those cause some irrational agitation. One person wrote me: "I am sorry but that performance is nothing amazing. I would say it's ok, but not great."

Don't hate, congratulate! That critic's thinking is not very bright. Passive aggressive you could say.

Better yet, consider compounding some of these numbers. For example, if you could make 50 percent a year, you could compound an initial $20,000 account to more than $616,000 in just seven years. Is 50 percent unrealistic? Of course it is. However, do the math again using 25 percent.

> Compound interest is the 8th wonder of the world.[17]

Think about this: Since October 1997, one trend following trader has produced annualized returns higher than 21 percent. To put that in context, if you bought Vincent van Gogh's Irises in 1947, you paid $80,000. The next time it changed hands, in 1987, it was sold for $53.9 million. That seems like a huge increase in value, but mathematically it shows a compound average annual growth rate of 17.7 percent, which is less than the annualized returns of my example trend trader.[18]

One of the first Wall Street books I ever read was Jim Rogers' *Investment Biker*. Rogers brought much passion and common sense to the table. Nearly 14 years later, in early 2008, my travels took me to see him at his home in Singapore for my documentary film. Rogers, who is not a technical trend following trader, but who has made a fortune trading trends, put the importance of compounding at the top of his list:

> "One of the biggest mistakes most investors make is believing that they've always got to be doing something. The trick to investing is not to lose money. The losses will kill you. They ruin your compounding rate; and compounding is the magic of investing."[19]

You can perform yourself out of business.

Why is trend following money making not common knowledge for so many? The journey to find that answer is not a straight line.

Hello? Is there anybody in there?
Just nod if you can hear me.
Is there anyone at home?[1]

Blowing Bubbles

"People are shortsighted, overconfident in so-called predictive skills, and irrationally prone to buying insurance on cheap home appliances. In short, they exhibit tendencies not unlike your not so swift brother-in-law."

"The human brain responds to high-stakes trading just as it does to the lure of sex. And the riskier trades get, the more the brain craves them."

"Social conformity drives human beings. Even if the group is wrong, people go along."

Sounds about right, right? Consider the question: Does raw human emotion dictate financial decisions, or are we rational calculators of our self-interest?

The idea that we behave irrationally when it comes to money may not seem radical, but it challenges the dominant University of Chicago economic philosophy that has framed business and government for fifty years. Their campus has given rise to more Nobel Prize winners in economics than any other institution. Nearly all share the common assumption: When it comes to money, we are highly rational.[3]

> At the peak of tulip mania in Holland, in February 1637, single tulip bulbs sold for more than 10 times the annual income of a skilled craftsman.[2]

One of the foremost champions of that view is Gary Becker: "The most powerful theory we have, and I think it's the most powerful theory in the social sciences, is economics as a theory of rational behavior at an individual level, and that's the theory we rely on."[4]

Other academics are not on board for obvious reasons: "The 2008 crash really matters because much of the behavior that led up to the crash is unexplained by the discipline of economics."[5]

> Beware of consensus.

More Chicago academics ignore the 2008 crash: "I'm sorry, that's such an empty argument. That's just an insult, a pointless insult."[6] Eugene Fama, the father of so-called efficient markets, smirked: "I don't see this as a failure of economics, but we need a whipping boy, and economists have always been whipping boys, so they're used to it. It's fine."[7]

Those economists defend their view no matter what. People and markets are rational? Small children now know that is not true. However, university professors have convinced themselves human beings only use robotlike logic.

On the other hand, Jeremy Grantham has made money for 40 years by finding price bubbles and betting against them: "We've found 27 bubbles. It's euphoria causing the price to go up and realism causing it to fall back, and then, eventually, unrealistic panic, as it begins to feed on itself, and the lemmings head in the opposite direction."[8]

One academic does see it like Grantham. Nobel Prize winner Vernon Smith devised an experimental market in which investors could create a financial "bubble." Far from learning from their experience after creating a bubble, investors would go on to create yet another bubble. This time, the bubble occurred earlier than the prior experiment and was not as pronounced as the first. When investors were asked why they allowed themselves to create a second bubble, the most common response was they thought they could get out before the top *this* time. Smith's research showed that the only reliable method of removing bubbles is to use players who are experienced twice over. We apparently only learn after two blowups![9]

Give Rod Serling credit for figuring *it* all out back in 1960, and give him more credit for burying it so illusively in an episode of *The Twilight Zone*:

> **Alien visitor #1:** Understand the procedure now? Just stop a few of their machines and radios and telephones and lawn mowers...throw them into darkness for a few hours, and then just sit back and watch the pattern.
>
> **Alien visitor #2:** And this pattern is always the same?
>
> **Alien visitor #1:** With few variations. They pick the most dangerous enemy they can find and it's...themselves. All we need to do is sit back...and watch.[10]

> 100-year floods actually happen far more frequently. Since 1929 there have been 18 market crashes.[11]

Popular delusions are a foundation of trend following profit.

The mother of all evil
is speculation.[1]

The most valuable
commodity I know of
is information,
wouldn't you agree?[2]

Note: Those two quotes are from film director Oliver Stone.

Speculari

The film director Oliver Stone believes that speculation is evil. That's *interesting*. He has written some fantastic scripts. He has directed Oscar-winning films. Nevertheless, to say that speculation is "the mother of all evil" is disingenuous. When Stone sets forward to make a new film, he's speculating that you will spend your money and watch his film. There is nothing wrong with that. That's life. That's a good thing.

Speculation in markets is essential too. Think about what drives a market. It is millions of people speculating to make money. One of the most successful trend following traders knows deep down how important speculation is to finding opportunity:

> Why did the market fall? There was more selling than buying.

> "*Speculari*, the Latin root of the verb "to speculate" has the literal meaning to observe. To be successful this observation must, of necessity, be detached and unemotive and thus where great social and moral issues are at stake, it is perhaps not surprising that distrust and hostility among the general population can arise particularly when the speculator profits at a time of general discontent. Yet this detached observation is clearly in the spirit of the natural scientist and the act of speculating for money is in the spirit of the empirical scientist's restless yearning to add to empirical knowledge and put theories to the test."[3]

Regardless of whether you win or lose, you are speculating—trying to get ahead. Every time you get into a car, you are speculating. If you go to the Apple store to buy an iPhone you are speculating the phone is more valuable than your dollars. Additionally, you are speculating the iPhone will work. When you turn on a show you are speculating that it is worth more than something else. All of these activities don't always work out, and that is the nature of speculation. All speculators are not winners.[4]

So why is it bad to take advantage of an opportunity that you recognize? It's not.

Speculate this: Do you consider yourself an investor or a trader? Investors put their money into investments hoping value will increase over time. Typically, they have no plan if it goes down. They usually hold on, praying value will reverse and go back up. Investors typically succeed in bull markets and lose in bear markets. They usually have no coherent response when the losing starts. They often hang tight and continue to lose even more.

> The law of gravity:
> What goes up
> must also
> come down.

Traders are different. They have a defined strategy to put money to work for a single goal: profit. Wise trend traders do not care what they buy or sell as long as they end up with more money in the long run. Bottom line, winning traders don't invest, they trade. It is a massive distinction.

Consider timeless qualities essential to speculation:

1. Self-reliance: A man must think for himself and must follow his own convictions. Self-trust is the foundation of successful effort.
2. Judgment: That equipoise, that nice adjustment of the faculties of one to the other, which is called good judgment—essential to the speculator.
3. Courage: That is, confidence to act on the decisions of the mind. In speculation, there is value in the dictum: Be bold, still be bold; always be bold.
4. Prudence: The power of measuring the danger, together with a certain alertness and watchfulness, is very important. There should be a balance of prudence and courage; prudence in contemplation, courage in execution.

> Recent college graduates have
> structured their lives around
> speculation that a high-paying
> job awaits following graduation.
> That's not very smart
> speculation.[6]

5. Pliability: The ability to change an opinion, the power of revision. He who observes and observes again is always formidable.[5]

I don't care whether you ever trade, but those precepts should be the first life lessons taught to grade school kids.

My own view is that this planet is used as a penal colony, lunatic asylum, and dumping ground by a superior civilization, to get rid of the undesirable and unfit. I can't prove it, but you can't disprove it either. It happens to be my view, but it doesn't challenge any of the findings of Darwin or Huxley or Einstein or Hawking.[1]

Fundamentals Are Religion

There are two basic market theories. The fundamentalist studies economic realities—supply and demand factors—that they believe underlie market values. Fundamental analysis relies on government policy, economic projections, price-earnings ratios, and balance sheet analysis (and so on) to make buy and sell decisions. The religion of fundamental analysis is about telling *stories*:

- Crude oil traded near an eight-week low because of concern fuel demand will be curbed amid signs of slowing economic growth in the U.S. and the U.K.
- History suggests the time is right to buy Dow stocks.
- It's not too late to profit from rally as market's cycle shifts in favor of blue-chip stocks.
- They're cheap by recent historical standards.
- The index's trailing price to earnings ratio, a measure that shows investors how much they are paying for a dollar in earnings, is well below what it has averaged.
- The price to earnings ratio for the S&P 500.
- Commodities look to be more expensive in the coming sessions and coming weeks to months.
- Has the metals correction run its course?
- My gut tells me the indices are overdue for a setback but the jury is still out.
- Secular decline over the last four cycles.
- We feel an interim top is in.
- Decline in nominal GDP.
- Based on supply and demand constraints, corn and soybeans need to trade higher to ration demand and to find more acreage.
- Initial unemployment claims.
- Is this just a correction or could it turn into something more serious?
- Political and social unrest in the Middle East.

- Big miss in headline payrolls.
- Key driver of seasonal demand patterns in gold.
- A bullish USDA report aided in corn appreciation.
- Rising energy and materials shares, spurred by surging oil and gold prices, have kept stocks in positive territory.
- The FOMC is meeting today and tomorrow so stay alert as even inaction can be a market mover.
- EBITDA.

> **The system wins. Fundamentals are nice, but useless in trading. True fundamentals are always unknown.[2]**

The fundamentals never stop. So do you buy or sell oil now? Exactly. Who knows how to really trade with fundamentals? Very few, if any, know how to use them.

This is not new. People have told stories for centuries. It is an activity that calms and soothes. Think about religions. Many were created to satiate a desire for order. Investors are no different. They want "cause and effect" explanations and feel security in the illusion that there is a deeper understanding. It does not matter if the moneymaking strategy works or not. All that matters is the story. Sheep go to slaughter much easier when they're comforted and showered with sweet nothings.

So how can the religion of fundamental analysis, taught on every college campus and practiced at every mutual fund, generate repeatable alpha? It cannot.

> **They said the market's wrong. It'll come back. The market is never wrong.**

Example. One famed financial web site pointed to chocolate pudding in their bio. When they were young, they learned about stocks from their father at the supermarket. He would say, "See that pudding? We own the company that makes it. Every time someone buys that pudding, it's good for our company. So go get some more."[3]

That story might be cute, but it is childlike ideology. Krispy Kreme makes great donuts (no doubt), but it's stock is around $6 years after reaching a high of more than $40 a share. The "story" is irrelevant.

However, even the so-called educated don't see clearly. A billion dollar fund invited me to talk. They wanted to invest money into trend following but were having a hard time accepting that it was not rooted in fundamentals. They were comfortable with a trader who *knew* one market alone—fundamentally. They worshipped the idea that a trader could know everything about some one market, which would supposedly translate to profit. They could not grasp trend following.

It does not matter if you're trading stocks or soybeans. Trading is trading, and the name of the game is to make money, not get an A in "How to Read a Balance Sheet."[5]

> If a market is going up you go long; if it is going down, you go short.
> The only reason you take a trade is because the market is doing something.[4]

Technical analysis, the other market theory, operates in stark contrast. It is based on the belief that at any given point in time, market prices reflect all known fundamentals for that particular market. Instead of trying to evaluate fundamental factors, technical analysis looks at market prices themselves.

There are essentially two forms of technical analysis. The first is based on reading charts and using indicators to supposedly predict market direction. For example, here is a mixing of fundamentals and predictive technical analysis:

> The illusion has been created that there is an explanation for everything with the primary task to find that explanation.[6]

Grains all made subtle bull breakout technical moves last week as continued fear of a global grain panic builds premium into these markets. I do believe that the grain rally should be sold into as it will be short-lived in 2011. The market is in the "what-if" stage of the winter season as they get ready for plantings. What if China needs to import corn? What if Australia's wheat crop is gone? What if cotton acreage squeezes beans? Well how about what if the market meets demand? I do not expect grain prices to test 2008 levels—the fundamentals are not there yet and the hype isn't strong enough. Soybeans are a good spread play against corn, but overall I would be a put buyer across the board. Rice is a sell into this short covering rally with straight puts.

That is a view of technical analysis held by many. It's worthless. Run when you see that kind of talk.

Yet, there is another type of technical analysis that does not try to predict. Trend followers are the traders who use *reactive* technical analysis. They react to market movements and follow along—without a story.

You can mix fundamental
analysis with trend following.
You can mix it with astrology,
four-leaf clovers,
chicken bones, lucky crickets,
and Aunt May's arthritis cure.
But why would you?
Except to give the
appearance that there's
a special sauce to
trend trading.[7]

A prophet is not
someone with special
vision, just blind to
what others see.[1]

Everything Flows

What is a trend? The question has hit me for over a decade. You don't *spot* trends. You don't *find* trends. You react to market movements, and hopefully at the end of a big move, a big trend, you will have made great money from that big trend.

Watch chart lines... not headlines.

Consider an example to better make my point. A new trader asked: "I am new to trend following and wish to ask you what your favorite chart is for determining a given market's trend? Daily, weekly, yearly, hourly?"

One old pro trend trader responded: "Your list lacks options for minute, second, and millisecond. If you want to go for the really high-frequency stuff, you might try trading visible light, in the range of one cycle per 10-15 seconds. Trading gamma rays, at around one cycle per 10-20 seconds, requires a lot of expensive instrumentation, whereas you can trade visible light by eye. Higher-frequency trading succumbs to declining profit potential against non-declining transaction costs. You might consider trading a chart with a long enough time scale that transaction costs are a minor factor—something like a daily price chart, going back a year or two."[2]

All trends are historical. None are in the present. There is no way to determine a current trend, or even define what current trend might mean. You can only determine historical trends. And the only way to measure a *now* trend, one entirely in the moment of now, would be to take two points, both in the now and compute their difference. However, with that limitation in mind, you can proceed to define, compute, and use trends.[3]

Trends in motion will stay in motion, they will persist, until they reverse.[4]

That's no philosophical word smithing. It is critical that you let the distinctions sink in.

You don't need to know what will happen next in order to profit from whatever happens next.

Systematic Trend Following

What is trend following trading? The first part is *trend*. That is very straightforward. Every trader needs a trend to make money. *Following* is part two of the phrase. Trend followers wait for a market to move first and then they follow it.[1]

Now, some argue that the term *trend following* is too imprecise. Others use terms like *global statistical financial analysis* or *managed futures* to describe the strategy. That debate will not be solved here. If you do not like the phrase trend following, substitute your term as you keep reading.

Trend following trading is reactive. It does not predict market direction. Trend trading demands self-discipline to follow precise rules (no guessing or wild emotions). It involves a certain risk management that uses the current market price, equity level in your account, and current market volatility.

> We decided that systematic trading was best. Fundamental trading gave me ulcers.[2]

Trend traders use an initial risk rule to determine their trading size at entry. That means you know exactly how much to buy or sell based on how much money you have. Changes in price may lead to a gradual reduction or increase of your initial trade. On the other hand, adverse price movements will lead to an exit. A trend trader's average profit per trade is significantly higher than the average loss per trade.

Trend following aims to capture the middle, or the meat, of a market trend, up or down, for profit. You will never get in at the absolute bottom or get out at the absolute top. Stocks, ETFs, LEAPS options, bonds, currencies, futures, and commodities are all ripe to trade.

This is the only trading strategy that can be traded on a desert island. As long as price data is available, all else is inconsequential. Media, fundamentals, broker opinions, talking heads, and so on are simply not necessary to profit.

Yes, initial discretionary decisions must be made as a trend follower, such as choosing a trend following system, selecting a portfolio, and determining an appropriate amount to risk. However, after the basics have been set in motion, you can systematize trend-trading rules and automate your daily trading life. This is not day trading, where you are glued to the screen all day in some Red Bull®–induced hyperactivity bender.

> Trend following works because you don't outthink it. You are a follower, not a predictor.[3]

However, you have to maintain agnosticism to market direction for trend trading success. Unfortun-ately, not everyone comprehends or wants to comprehend that.

Consider Erin Burnett of CNBC. She was interviewing David Harding—a successful trend trader—and asked: "A lot of people obviously want to know what your secret is. What was the magic bullet?"

Harding replied: "The secret strangely enough is not having an idea of what we are going to be doing in advance. We react to the unfolding markets trends rather than make forecasts of what's going to happen."

> The market is not the economy and the market has no sympathy for you, your family, or your emotions. It might not be fair, it might not be right, but it is what it is.[4]

Burnett missed his point in response: "When you look out right now do you think, big picture, I know you are quantitative, but do you believe that we are in a fundamental cycle or are we in a bubble?"

Harding: "It's not false modesty for me to say I don't know. I really don't know. I really do not have the gift of second sight."

Consider fundamental investor John Hussman. His writings are always insightful. He makes a cogent case for an out of control Fed and Congress, but consider an excerpt from his recent letter:

> "In hindsight, I frankly underestimated the willingness of investors to believe that the underlying structural difficulties of the economy (which still persist in my view) were so easily solved by disabling fair-market accounting disclosure and repeatedly violating the provisions of the Federal Reserve Act. In any event, it is my job to not only defend capital, but to achieve returns despite the recklessness that policy makers choose to pursue."[5]

> Ride the horse in the direction it is going.[6]

Trend traders use an entirely different type of analysis not based on traditional reasoning. Trend followers do not have Hollywood narratives to explain market bubbles on top of bubbles. A trend follower does not have to know any of the things Hussman laments not knowing.

> Buy things that have gone up on the theory that they will continue to go up; short things that have gone down on the theory that they will continue to go down.[7]

Empty your mind. Be formless, shapeless, like water. Now you put water into a cup, it becomes the cup. You put water into a bottle it becomes the bottle. You put it in a teapot it becomes the teapot. Now water can flow or it can crash. Be water, my friend.[1]

Change

Markets go up, down, and sideways. They trend. They flow. They surprise.

Have markets changed? Not only have markets changed, they will continue to change. Check your history books. If you have a valid market philosophy, learning to accept that change and flow with it is your greatest asset. No matter how ridiculous market moves appear at the beginning, and no matter how extended or irrational they seem at the end, following trends is the rational choice in a chaotic, changing world.[2]

That thinking leaves trend followers as generalists when it comes to their trading strategy and that's not easy to accept for many. The dominant *trend* within universities is ever-narrower specialization. A higher premium is placed on deep knowledge within a single field (read: fundamental expertise in one market), versus broad wisdom across multiple fronts.[3]

> Trend following doesn't argue with markets.

For example, one trend following practitioner started trading trends in 1974—making hundreds of millions in profits and perhaps billions for clients. The major strategic elements of his trend following trading systems have never changed. He was blunt: "The markets are just the markets. I know that is unusual sounding."[4]

Occasionally, someone trying to promote something or start a debate will argue that trend following has to change due to changing market conditions. Specious. The root of trend following is based on responding to change. It is designed to be adaptable.

Does that mean every systematic trend trader will take the risk of shooting only for huge returns? No. Does that mean every trend trader will capture a trend in the exact same way? No. The trend following *way* has many practitioners and many recipes. However, just as there are thousands of car models, they are still cars.

> The market will fluctuate.[5]

Prediction is very difficult, especially about the future.

No Prediction

"There are many, many things that Google could do, that we choose not to do. One day we had a conversation where we figured we could just try to predict the stock market. And then we decided it was illegal. So we stopped doing that."[1]

Google is a great search engine. It won the title of search king, and former CEO Eric Schmidt has made a fortune. Congratulations. However, when he opines like that, he sounds delusional. Schmidt might be worth billions, but wealth does not make up for a lack of common sense.

He is one of many.

> Prices predict the future, not investors.

A group of *eminent* economists recently apologized to Queen Elizabeth II for failing to predict the financial crisis: "In summary, your majesty, the failure to foresee the timing, extent and severity of the crisis and to head it off, while it had many causes, was principally a failure of the collective imagination of many bright people, both in this country and internationally, to understand the risks to the system as a whole."

What did the Queen think when she received that? Did she believe it? Did she know better? No one can absolutely know when a market will move and trend. Do you have to know to profit? No.

Look at insurance, gambling, and other related businesses. It is clear that even a small positive *edge*, along with a solid view of probabilities, can lead to fortunes. However, that does not mean the path to prosperity will necessarily be comfortable.

Think about the emotional ups and downs when facing the unknown. Leaving Las Vegas recently, I drove down toward Hoover Dam. Knowing I would soon be from the vantage point of the new Hoover Dam bridge spanning the Colorado River, the feeling of anxiety was encompassing. During the decline, you do not know how far you will be able to see down, but when you finally get to the bridge, you can't actually see the dam over the ledge! The wall is too high. Relief.[2]

That is the life of a trend trader too: Keeping in check how you react to the unexpected or unknowable. Many trend traders have even gone back and looked at 19th century markets to see if their strategies would have been successful. Interest rates, currencies, and grain prices in the 1800s showed just as many trends. The markets were as random and unpredictable as today.[3]

Similar research took me to the National Agricultural Library in Beltsville, Maryland. My curiosity had me walking stacks reviewing 1800s historical price data from the *Economist* magazine. I verified the same price data research—indeed, unpredictable trends were across all markets.

Fast forward 100 years and consider a story about a trading seminar where a notable trend follower was the guest speaker. The audience peppered him with questions: "Do you like gold?" "Where do you think the Canadian dollar is headed?" "How do you know when there is a top?" To each of these, he replied: "I like gold, its shiny, pretty, makes nice jewelry" or "I have no idea where the Canadian dollar is headed." Many were not impressed. They felt they had wasted their money. However, his message could not have clearer. The answers were found in the very questions each person asked. Do not ask, "How do you know the trend is moving up?" Instead, ask, "What is going to tell me the trend is up?" Not, "What do you think of gold?" Instead, ask, "Am I correctly trading gold?"[4]

> Long term trend following is about survival.

His answers placed everyone in front of a mirror and worse yet, some did not know it.

It's gettin' so a businessman can't expect no return from a fixed fight. Now, if you can't trust a fix, what can you trust? For a good return, you gotta go bettin' on chance and then you're back with anarchy, right back in the jungle.[1]

Price Action

Tell me something the "market" does not know.

The idea that you can know enough about Apple, oil, GE, and gold to trade them all the same way may seem preposterous, but think about what they all have in common:

Price.

Market price is objective data. You can look at individual price histories, without knowing which market is which, and still trade all successfully. That is not what they teach at Harvard, Wharton, Kellogg, Stern, Darden, or pick your favorite business school du jour.

> Don't guess how far a trend will go. You cannot. Price makes the news, not the other way around.
> A market is going to go where a market is going to go.[2]

However, the concept of price as the critical trading cue may be too simple for mass acceptance. For example, a prominent business anchor opined: "At some point, investing is an act of faith. If you can't believe the numbers, annual reports, etc., what numbers can you believe?"

A longtime financial reporter at *Fortune* magazine was also on the highway going the wrong direction: "If some of the smartest people on Wall Street can't trust the numbers, you wonder who can trust the numbers."[3]

> The best estimate of tomorrow's price is today's price.

You can never trust those *numbers*—that is, the reported firm details—completely. Someone can always alter them (remember Enron had a fake trading floor). Beyond that, even if you know accurate balance sheet numbers, how does this help you determine when or how much to buy or sell?

The market is always right, and price is the only true reality in trading. If you want to make money in any market, you need to mirror what the market is doing. If the market is going down and you are long, the market is right and you are wrong. If the market is going up and you are short, the market is right and you are wrong. Other things being equal, the longer you stay right with the market, the more money you will make. The longer you stay wrong with the market, the more money you will lose.[4]

You do not need to know anything about bonds. You do not need to understand different currencies. They are just numbers. Corn is a little different than bonds, but not different enough to trade them differently. Some people have a different system for each market. That is absurd. You are trading mob psychology. You are not trading corn, soybeans, or S&P's. You are merely trading numbers.[5]

**Price is fact;
all else conjecture.**

This is not Groupon®.
No risk, no reward.

Place Your Bet

You want to see life as a continuum running on a loop back and forth from risk to reward. If you want a big reward, take a big risk. If you want an average reward and an average life, take an average risk. Easier said than done, however, if you want the big reward. Our *system* is notorious for playing Whac-A-Mole with achievers.

From an early age, people are conditioned by families, schools, and virtually every other shaping force in society to avoid risk. To take risks is inadvisable; to play it safe is the message. Risk can only be bad. However, winners understand risk is highly productive, and not something to avoid. Taking calculated risks is different from acting rashly. Playing it safe is the true danger. Far more often than you might realize, the real risk in life turns out to be the refusal to take a risk.[2]

> Give me a lever long enough and a fulcrum on which to place, and I shall move the world.[1]

If life is a game of risk, then to one degree or another, being comfortable with assessing odds is the only option for a fulfilling life.

Consider trading from a "startup" business perspective. Every business is ultimately involved in assessing risk. Putting capital to work to make it grow is the goal. In that sense, all business is the same. The right decisions lead to success, and wrong ones lead to insolvency.

> Return and risk are the two sides of the same coin.

Blunt, but true.

There are ways to go in the right direction, however. Ask yourself these questions:

- What is the market opportunity in the market niche?
- What is your solution to the market need?
- How big is the opportunity?
- How do you make money?
- How do you reach the market and sell?
- What is the competition?
- How are you better?

- How will you execute and manage your business?
- What are your risks?
- Why will you succeed?

Those questions are just the start of your trend following journey. The next step is thinking deeply about your understanding of risk nuances.

There are two kinds of risk: blind and calculated. The first one, blind risk, is always suspect. Blind risk is the calling card of laziness: the irrational hope, something for nothing, the cold twist of fate, winning the lottery, etc. Blind risk is the pointless gamble, the emotional decision, or the sucker play. The man who embraces blind risk never wins in the long run.

However, calculated risk can build fortunes, nations, and empires. Calculated risk and bold vision go hand in hand. To see the possibilities, work things out logically, and to move forward in strength and confidence is how you win. Calculated risk lies at the heart of every great achievement and achiever since the dawn of time.

Don't bet your deli to win a pickle.[3]

Trend followers thrive on taking calculated risks. Like the original *Karate Kid* movie: Wax on, wax off. Risk on, risk off.

Jake: The band? The band.

Reverend Cleophus James: Do you see the light?

Jake: The band!

Reverend Cleophus James: Do you see the light?

Elwood: What light?

Reverend Cleophus James: Have you seen the light?

Jake: Yes! Yes! Jesus H. Tap-Dancing Christ... I have seen the light![1]

Trading Systems

You want to see the *light*? Trading coach Charles Faulkner paints a picture:

- No one can predict the future.
- If you can take the would-be, could-be, should-be out of life and look at what actually is, you have a big advantage over most human beings.
- What matters can be measured, so keep refining your measurements.
- You don't need to know when something will happen to know that it will.
- Prices can only move up, down, or sideways.
- Losses are a part of life.
- There is only now.[2]

Now, let's get practical. Answer the following five questions, and you have a trend following trading system:

1. What market do you buy or sell at any time?
2. How much of a market do you buy or sell at any time?
3. When do you buy or sell a market?
4. When do you get out of a losing position?
5. When do you get out of a winning position?

    Said another way:

1. What is the state of the market?
2. What is the volatility of the market?
3. What is the equity being traded?
4. What is the system or the trading orientation?
5. What is the risk aversion of the trader or client?[3]

You want to be black or white with this. You do not want gray. If you can accept that mentality, you have got *it*.

Some might say, "Oh, I have a system." What he typically means is that he has a system, and it advises him what to do. If he likes the advice, he'll take it, and if he doesn't like the advice, he won't take it. That is not science. You cannot test or simulate how you were feeling when you got out of bed 15 years ago when you're looking at historical simulations. If you're going to

Since the 1970s, and earlier, simple systems have demonstrated an ability to generate outstanding returns.[5]

trade using a system, you must slavishly use the system and avoid discretionary overrides. You do whatever the hell the system says no matter how smart or dumb you might think it is at that moment.[4]

Trend following systems can vary, but principle elements remain the same. A reversal system, a very common system, has two modes: You are either long or short. It is always in the market. It closes one position by opening a new one in the opposite direction.

Another type of system has three-phases adding a third mode: neutral, where you are not in the market. If you are long, and you get an exit signal, you don't necessarily go short automatically. You can be out of the market. Here are concrete trend following system examples to start you on the path:

- You can either be long or short at any time. You enter a long position (and exit a short position) if the current price exceeds the highest price in the previous 100 days. You enter a short position (and exit a long position) if the current price drops below the lowest price in the previous 100 days. You are positioned either long or short in each market at all times depending on the direction of the prevailing trend.[6]

- You allocate risk, and size your position based on each market's historical volatility. Each market receives an equal allocation of the total portfolio risk. Position sizes are normalized based on their volatility. The measure of volatility that you use is called the Average True Range. The size of your position you take in any given market is dependent only upon the individual market's volatility and the total account value, that is, it is independent of any other market's volatility or position in your portfolio.[7]

- You buy when a market makes a new four-week high or sell when it makes a new four-week low. If you are long, you go short if it makes a new four-week low. If you are short, you go long if it makes a new four-week high.

- You can find more systems in my book *The Complete TurtleTrader* and in *Technical Traders Guide to Computer Analysis of the Futures Markets* by Charles Lebeau.

Those are sound trend following systems. There are variations and nuances across the trend following world, but when big trends happen you need to have an approach that can get you on board, and simple often works best. The absolute key is, and this will never register with skeptics and critics, your discipline to stick with your system. That will always far out-weigh whether you have the per-fect set of entry and exit rules.

Further, many argue that money management is far more important than your entry-exit

> **The markets have not changed. They were constantly changing then just as they are constantly changing now.[8]**

rules. Further yet, portfolio selection is often argued to be much more important than your money management. Keep an open eye to this. Don't get rigid.

Let me clarify money management. Money management, also called risk management, position sizing, and bet sizing, is crucial. It is like sex: Everyone does it, one way or another, but most do not want to talk about it, and some do it better than others. When you make a decision to buy or sell (short), you also decide at that time how many shares or contracts to buy or sell. Accept too much risk and you increase the odds that you will go bust; take too little risk and you will not be rewarded sufficiently.[9]

Posit the question, "I've only got a certain amount of money. How much do I trade?" If you have $100,000 and you want to trade Microsoft, well, how much of your $100,000 will you trade of Microsoft on your first trade? Will you trade all $100,000? What if you're wrong? What if you're wrong in a big way, and you lose your entire $100,000 on one bet? Not smart.

How do you determine how much to bet or trade each time? Trend fol-lowers make small bet sizes initially. So, if you start at $100,000, and you're going to risk 2 percent, that will be $2,000. You might say to yourself, "I've got $100,000, why am I only risking $2,000? $2,000 is nothing." That's not the point. You can't predict anything, so you have to be worried about your downside, not your upside.

Risking no more than 1 percent per trade is a good place to start, and risking more than 5 percent per trade is a sure way to the poor house.[10]

There is a tradeoff as you ponder how much to risk. Conservative betting produces conservative performance, while bold betting can lead to spectacu-lar ruin. A bold trader placing large bets feels pressure or "heat" from the volatility of a portfolio. A "hot" portfolio keeps more at risk than does a cold one. A portfolio risking 2 percent on each of five instruments has a total heat of 10 percent, as does a portfolio risking 5 percent on each of two instruments.[11]

However, once you select a system, and once you have your money man-agement thought through, no less critical is your attitude:

- What do you really want?
- Why are you trading?
- What are your strengths and weaknesses?
- Do you have any emotional issues?
- How disciplined are you?
- Are you easily convinced?
- How confident are you in yourself?
- How confident are you in your system?
- How much risk can you handle?

Those are personal questions. I can't answer them for you.

Note: Do yourself a favor and read the free document online titled "Determining Optimal Risk" by Dave Druz and Ed Seykota. It is a great starting point for taking your money management education further.

A trend following system with an edge allows a smart "betting" scheme to amplify profits.[12]

The thesis is simple:
The world is chaotic.

Trade Everything

What you trade is critical. It may just be the most important issue.

Here is the conundrum: You cannot trade everything, but you cannot trade only one market either. You need to be in a position to be following enough markets that when a market moves you can ride it, as diversification is the only free lunch you get. It allows you to spread your potential targets of opportunity broadly across currencies, interest rates, global stock indices, grains, softs (wheat, cotton, etc.), meats, metals, and energies.

You do not need to know the market's name. They are all the same when you look at price data only. If they are all the same, then

> In order for a trend trading strategy to be accepted it must trade all markets using the same rules. There should be excellent performance for the vast majority of markets.[1]

an opportunistic strategy that is ready to go when a trend starts can make you serious money. That's how the fortunes discussed in the earlier chapter "Show Me the Money" were made.

The following is an example of a diversified portfolio that you could use as a starting point for assembling your own portfolio (with the exchanges listed where markets are traded):

British Pound (CME; www.cmegroup.com)

Canadian Dollar (CME)

Euro (CME)

Swiss Franc (CME)

Japanese Yen (CME)

Australian Dollar (CME)

Mexican Peso (CME)

Eurodollar (CME)

Euribor (NYSE LIFFE; www.euronext.com)

Aussie Bank Bills (ASX; www.asx.com.au)

U.S. 10-Year Note (CME)

U.S. 30-Year Bond (CME)

Canadian Gov't. Bond (CME)

Long Gilt (NYSE LIFFE)

Euro-German Bond (EUREX; www.eurexchange.com)

JGB (TSE; www.tse.or.jp)

Aussie 10-Year Bond (ASX)

Wheat (CME)

Wheat (KCBT; www.kcbt.com)

Corn (CME)

Soybeans (CME)

Soy Meal (CME)

Bean Oil (CME)

Canola (ICE; www.theice.com)

Cotton (ICE)

Sugar (ICE)

London Sugar (NYSE LIFFE)

Coffee (ICE)

Coffee Robusta (NYSE LIFFE)

Cocoa (ICE)

Cocoa (NYSE LIFFE)

Orange Juice (ICE)

Milk (CME)

Lumber (CME)

S&P 500 Mini (CME)

Russell 2000 Mini (CME)

FTSE 100 (NYSE LIFFE)

Nikkei (SGX; www.sgx.com)

Euro Stoxx 50 (EUREX)

Hang Seng (HKEX; www.hkex.com.hk)

Australian SPI 200 (ASX)

Lean Hogs (CME)

Live Cattle (CME)

Feeder Cattle (CME)

Platinum (CME)

Silver (CME)

Gold (CME)

HG Copper (CME)

Aluminum (LME; www.lme.com)

Nickel (LME)

Zinc (LME)

Light Crude Oil (CME)

Brent Crude Oil (ICE)

Heating Oil (CME)

Gas Oil (ICE)

Unleaded Gas (CME)

Natural Gas (CME)[2]

That's diversity, and anyone can trade those markets today using Exchange Traded Funds (ETFs) or futures markets. If you say you can't, you are making excuses.

> It's one thing to calculate your risk on any one trade, but you live and die by the sum of multiple risk factors, which is why you calculate your portfolio risk too.[3]

Everyone is a loser
in the markets. No one wins.
Everyone is destined to be
scared hiding under their bed.
Then you die.
Life sucks, eh?

Drawdown

In the early 1990s, Commodities Corporation (a famed trading incubator that taught and bankrolled new traders) invited a group of Japanese traders to its company for in-house training. One up-and-coming trader at

> Some "win" by searching nonstop for the "answer," even when they have it.

Commodities Corporation took his new friends to lunch. He told his guests how important risk management was, and to risk only 1 percent per trade. He was clear that experiencing small losses were part of his process to ultimately finding big winners. The Japanese traders, with puzzled looks on their faces, asked, "You have losses?"[1]

Ouch! Time for everyone regardless of country to learn about small losses, and to love them, even if that means your account will occasionally have drawdowns. What are drawdowns?

Drawdowns are those nonfun time periods where your small losses add up to reduce your account size. They happen. The key is to quickly and successfully recover from them by sticking with your trend trading system

> Some like losing, so they win by losing money. Case in point: slots in Vegas.

and waiting patiently for big trends to reappear, which let you get back to making new money again (and paying for all of those small losses).

How much can you lose? That's an important question to answer, and it comes down to the risk you take (which will vary by your personal choice). However, trend following is much easier to believe in when you consider the length of professional trend trading track records, especially the really long track records that offer proof of viability. That said, some will spend a lifetime trying to avoid any loss even though its impossible...as Chart 8 shows.

Chart 8: Trend Following Trader Sunrise Capital Compared to Largest Quarterly S&P Drawdowns

Time Period	Event	S&P 500 Index Performance	Sunrise Performance
1987 Q4	Black Monday	–23.23%	55.37%
2002 Q3	WorldCom Scandal	–17.63%	8.90%
2001 Q3	9-11	–14.99%	8.29%
1990 Q3	Iraq Invades Kuwait	–14.52%	41.21%
2002 Q2	Dot.Com Bubble	–13.73%	18.19%
2001 Q1	Tech Bear Market	–12.11%	11.22%
1998 Q3	Russian Default/LTCM	–10.30%	12.02%
2008 Q1	Credit Crisis	–9.92%	15.12%
2008 Q3	Credit Crisis/Bailout	–8.88%	–3.79%
2000 Q4	Dot.Com Bubble Burst	–8.09%	16.02%
1999 Q3	Y2K Anxiety	–6.56%	–0.98%
1994 Q1	Fed Rate Hikes	–4.43%	–4.55%
2007 Q4	Credit Crisis	–3.82%	13.46%
1990 Q1	Recession/Oil Spike	–3.81%	13.54%
2003 Q1	Second Gulf War	–3.60%	7.48%

Process versus outcome: Do you want to be right or rich?

Entry

"You really have no control over the results; you have control over the action."

To live that statement means accepting certain truths. For example, you might want to imagine that there is a miraculously perfect entry price where you buy low. The real world doesn't work that way. Great trend traders have not made their fortunes that way.

> "If facing in the right direction, all you have to do is keep on walking." That is a Japanese trend following proverb...or at least I made it one.

Look at a nontrading example. I bought an investment property in Spring 2003 for $900,000. In January 2008, it was assessed at $1.2 million, and it was put on the market at $1.3 million. Obviously, things did not go well for real estate in 2008, and the best offer was the original purchase price of $900,000. It eventually sold at $1,010,000, but that barely covered costs and was a meager return on investment.

The lesson: My original price was irrelevant. The only relevant number was what someone would pay for it today, or the market price. It does not matter how much you think you should get.

For example, if you enter a market at price level 50 and it goes to 100, does it really make a difference whether you got in at 52 or 60 or 70? Even if you got in at 70 and the market went to 100, you still made a lot, right? There are plenty of traders out there who think: "Oh, I couldn't get in at 52, so I won't get in at all." Even if you had the chance to get in at 70 on a market that eventually goes to 100, some sit on the sidelines still dreaming of buying 'cheap'!

Bottom line, entry is a very small concern—once you are in.[1]

Assume GOOG is trading between 500 and 550. All of a sudden GOOG jumps, or breaks out, to a price level of 600. That type of upward movement from a range is a trigger—the breakout for an entry. You might say, "I don't know if GOOG is going to continue up, but it's been going sideways for six months, and all of a sudden, the price has jumped to 600 making a new six-month highest high. I'm in."

You are not in this game to find bargains. You are in this to follow trends, and if the market is heading up, enter. If the market is heading down, enter short.

> The three best entry indicators in order are price, price, and price.

If trend trader Amos
Hostetter of Commodities
Corporation lost 25 percent,
he'd exit:
"Never mind the cheese.
Let me out of the trap."

This Way to the Egress

The paramount factor when the market goes against you is being able to say: "I'm out!" You need a *prenuptial agreement* with the market.[1]

That means the time to think most clearly about when you will exit is before you ever get in. A set in advance sell strategy gives you the opportunity to not only preserve capital (you need chips to play afterall), but to redeploy your limited capital to more favorable markets.

How do trend traders get out of a losing position? Fast! For example, you enter gold with a 2 percent stop loss. This means if you lose 2 percent, you exit. Period. Get out. There is no debate.

Think of it this way: If half of the time your trades go in your direction, you are hitting a good average. Even being right three or four times out of ten will yield a windfall if your losses are cut quickly when you are wrong.

You will never get in at the beginning of a trend or get out at the top. Picking tops and bottoms is not the objective. Think about the often-repeated phrase *profit targets*. Problem? They cap profits. For example, you enter some market at price level 100 and you decide that you will exit if the price hits 125. That may sound rational, but it is ignorant when re-eevaluated.

If you are riding a trend, you have to let it go as far as it can go. You need to fully exploit the length of the move. You do not want to exit at 125 and watch the trend go to 225.

> A new trader approached an old bold trend follower and asked, "What's your objective on this trade?" He replied, "For it to go to the moon."[2]

You need home run trends to pay for your small losses. If you are artificially creating a profit target for no other reason than comfort, you are prematurely stopping those potential big trends that actually get you rich. It's a vicious circle if you do not handle it properly from the beginning.

For example, you know your $50,000 account can go to $80,000, back to $55,000, back up to $90,000, and from there all the way up to $200,000. Take profits at $80,000 and you can't ride it up to $200,000. Letting profits *run* may feel counterintuitive psychologically, but trying to protect every penny of profit will actually prevent your big profits. Guaranteed.

Declare victory and get out. That means using stops and sticking to them.

**Forty percent of
Americans with
incomes less than
$35,000 a year believe
the lottery is their best chance
to make $500,000
for retirement.**

Losers Average Losers

There is a famous picture of a well-known trader relaxing in his office with his feet kicked up. A single sheet of loose-leaf paper is tacked on the wall behind him with the simple phrase written out in black marker:

"Losers Average Losers"

Trite meaningless talk? Not so fast.

Famed trader Jesse Livermore warned 100 years ago against averaging losses. For example, you buy a stock at 50 and two or three days later if you can buy it at 47, you average down by buying another hundred shares, making an average price of 48.5. Having bought at 50 and being concerned over a three-point loss on a hundred shares, what rhyme or reason is there in adding another hundred shares and having the double worry when the price hits 44? At that point, there would be a $600 loss on the first hundred shares and a $300 loss on the second shares. If you are able to apply such an unsound principle, you can keep on averaging down by buying 200 at 44, then 400 at 41, 800 at 38, 1600 at 35, 3200 at 32, 6400 at 29, and so on.[1]

> Escalator up, express elevator down.

"Don't frown, double down!" Not smart strategy.

Losses are a part of the game. You want no losses? You want positive returns every month? It does not work that way, that is, not unless you were lucky enough to be invested in the Bernard Madoff Ponzi-scheme—which has resulted in assorted criminal convictions and a few suicides.

Losses are not your problem. It's how you react to them. Ignore losses with no plan, or try to double down on your losses to recoup, and those losses will come back like a Mack truck to run over your account.

> You can't win if you are not willing to lose.
> It's like breathing in, but not breathing out.[2]

Slow everything down.
Don't compete with the phony speed
of society. Be a snake.
Coil and strike when the
time is right.

Home Run

Some companies, and individuals, stress the short-term performance of trend followers. They look at one month's performance, see a down month, and panic. They have complete ignorance of the long-term objective—big money.

How bad can it get? I have seen trend following traders make 100 percent in a year followed by a year where they lost 5 percent. That 5 percent loss causes some critics to not see the 100 percent number. That is insane thinking.

Just like a baseball player's batting average can have short-term up or down streaks over the course of a season, trend followers have streaks. Trend following performance will deviate from averages, but over time there is remarkable consistency when it comes to putting up big returns—as long as unpredictable home runs are allowed to happen naturally and unforced.

The leading thinkers across varied fields, including insurance, casino gambling, and investing, all emphasize the same point. It's the Babe Ruth effect: Even though Ruth struck out a lot, he was one of baseball's greatest hitters. The home runs made up for his strikeouts.[1]

A trend follower coaching a baseball team would approach it like the former manager of the Baltimore Orioles. Earl Weaver designed his offenses to maximize the chance of a three-run homer. Weaver did not bunt or want guys who slapped singles. He wanted guys who hit big home runs.[2]

> Trend followers are not front-running market opportunities; they follow them.

Trading is a waiting game. You sit, you wait, and you make a lot of money all at once. Profits come in bunches. The *trick* when going sideways between home runs is not to lose too much in between.[3]

Think about Madoff again. He fooled some of the United States' wealthiest individuals and charities. Mind you, I did not say America's smartest. Madoff knew one thing: He did not have to make big returns. All he had to do was fake 1 percent per month. That 1 percent per month was enough to satisfy believers.

I was at a conference in Brazil. My speaking time slot was on the second day. All the speakers, and this included many bright and accomplished people, kept lamenting how to spot the next Madoff. My simple answer: If an investment delivers 1 percent per month every month, with no down months, that investment is either a royal scam or a hidden disaster that will eventually blow up. Don't be snookered with consistency. Don't just believe—verify.

You should come to realize that trend following's unpredictable home runs are a much safer course of action.

Why didn't "brilliant" PhD economists sitting in the catbird seat see the **** storm in advance?

Robust

The occasional crank will whine this, or that. They always want it fast. They yearn for millions yesterday. I'll never understand why they can't relax and see that understanding and applying trend following takes time. It's not hard to digest conceptually, but it takes some time to understand the nuance and execute correctly.

For example, consider a high winning percentage. You've seen the carnival barkers on TV saying they've got a trading method that will make you a fortune because they have entry signals 90 percent accurate. Grab your wallet. It's about to be picked. You are about to be fleeced.

> All trend trading systems must hold up under as many different situations and market conditions as possible, and work as well no matter how markets evolve.[1]

A high percentage of winning trades should not be your focus. A need to be "right" misses the point. Pretend you trade 100 times in a year. The average winning trade makes you a net $100, and you make a net $9,000 for the winners. But the ten losing trades are for $1,000 each so you lose a total of $10,000 for the year in a system that had 90 percent winners. Not smart.[2]

That example leads to a broader issue behind trend following success. For a trend trading system to be successful, it needs to be robust. Assume you are trading Treasury Bonds and you switch to gold. Your system needs to still work. And if you switch to corn, something totally different from Treasury Bonds, it must work. Wear a loose-fitting suit. You can't have a suit so tight that if you gain two pounds it won't fit.[3]

To have a loose-fitting suit requires your trading system to be simple and intuitive. This means trend following rules that you could conceptually write down on the back of an envelope. If you can't do that, you can't win in the long run.

> Nobody can demonstrate that a complex mathematical equation can answer the simple question: Is the market moving up, down, or sideways?[4]

Today, we celebrate the first glorious anniversary of the information purification directives. We have created for the first time in all history a garden of pure ideology, where each worker may bloom, secure from the pests of any contradictory true thoughts. Our unification of thoughts is more powerful a weapon than any fleet or army on earth. We are one people, with one will, one resolve and one cause. Our enemies shall talk themselves to death and we will bury them with their own confusion. We shall prevail![1]

Push the Button

On January 24, 1984, Apple Computer introduced Macintosh. The advent of Apple has had its pros and cons. They have made life more fun for us. They have made life more organized. Yet they are still just tools. Computers do not think for us. Sure, a nice Mac or PC can help automate your life and make the daily grind easier, but they are no substitute for *thought*.

Great trend following traders know this. They take their trading rules and translate them into machine code to make life easier. If you have a new trading idea, a computer is the best tool for allowing you to see an idea applied over vast amounts of historical data. It puts our emotions to the side and makes testing *binary*.

> Means of market profits:
> Trend following rules + device + Internet cloud.

For example, if your boyfriend or girlfriend breaks up with you, you'll feel one subjective way unique to you. If you get engaged, you'll feel another way unique to your situation. The computer does not care, nor is it affected by your subejctive emotional whatever.[2]

Some retort back: "Why go the computer route if people power is so important?" It of course starts with people power, but great trend traders have proven that the computer route works. It is replicable—which equals confidence. If you have the same rules as someone else you can get similar results, and computers allow you to test that fast.[3]

Computers are not perfect though. You can easily overoptimize or curve fit a trading system, and produce a system that looks good on paper or screen alone. By testing thousands of possibilities, you can create a system that works in theory, but not the real world.

> It's cold, it's mathematical, and it's like a little robot. You push the button.

This, however, is all up against many competing messages. When you flip on the TV and see pitch men screaming at you (read: Wall Street "analysts"), causing instant aneurysms for the still sane, just remember "Red light! Green light! Two screens! Three screens!" is theatrics.

Human cogitation allows the creation of a great trend trading system, that's not loose sales talk or manic promises. Is there a risk that you mindlessly let the computer—like the machine in *War Games*—take over and do as it pleases? No. Do you change your trading system regularly? No, because your thinking and effort are behind the system you put into the computer.[4]

Pablo Picasso famously said, "Computers are useless. They can only give you answers." Start with your questions first. Automating your answers is the easy part.

A computer can let you evaluate 5,000 charts in the time it would take you to study 10 manually. However, if your original system is flawed, doing it wrong 500 times faster doesn't help.[5]

It's all a matter of perspective.
What some consider a catastrophic flood, others deem a cleansing bath.[1]

Wash, Rinse, Repeat

"Hey, I'm gonna get you too...another one bites the dust."

Another one really does bite the dust every few minutes. That does not mean a discussion of death, and of course people are dying, but rather millions are making horrendous decisions with their money (i.e., mutual funds, index investing, value investing, gurus, etc.). Further, if you think that you are going to get rich by listening to Dave Ramsey talking about decreasing your credit card debt, you got another thing coming.

With cable news and the Internet screaming information nonstop, every minute, all the time, people have just been conditioned to think events move too fast, and that they can't keep up or make winning decisions. Millions have thrown their hands up and screamed uncle.

I see it. I empathize. But you have to move on from *that*. You have to develop an understanding of how the game really works if you want to get ahead.

For example, Wall Street is known for corporate collapses and hedge fund blow-ups that transfer capital from winners to losers and back again. However, the winners always seem to be missing from the after-the-fact analysis. The press and the public are only fascinated with the losers. Everyone is oblivious to the other side of the story: the winners and why.

The academics locked away with job security tenure always come up short in their analysis: "It's a zero-sum game. For every loser there's a winner, but you can't always be specific about who the winner is."[2]

Not true.

> Bear markets cause events more than events cause bear markets.

John W. Henry made a fortune going short the Nikkei, while Nick Leeson and Barings Bank were long. That's a major winner right there.[3] My political science background allowed me to see *that*; others should be able to see it too.

However, many look at events through the wrong lens. Deep down the money elite know that standard finance theory has no explanation for the winners of low-probability, high-impact events.[4] The bottom line is that big, unexpected events make trend traders rich. They exploit *Black Swan* events (see Nassim Taleb's book of the same name for more).

What do I mean? When a major event occurs, such as the Russian debt default of August 1998, the terrorist attacks of September 11, 2001, or the 2002 and 2008 equity market crashes, events accelerate existing trends to even greater magnitudes.[5]

Unexpected events will never stop. People are people and there are always poor market strategies to exploit. Those with poor strategies are forever being cycled and recycled into the markets, giving continuous opportunities to capitalize on their missteps and take their money. And with so many people playing the big money game with such awful strategy, the next surprise win for trend following traders is right around the corner.

Isn't history littered with surprises?

**The new normal
is always
the old always.**

Zero-Sum

In a zero-sum game, someone can win only if somebody else loses.[1]

On any given market transaction, the chance of you winning or losing may be near even, but in the long run, you will only profit from trading because you have some persistent advantage (read: mathematical edge) that allows you to win slightly more often than losing.[2]

If you have ever played poker or studied edges in gambling, the words ring true: To trade profitably in the long run, you will know your edge, you will know when it exists, and you will exploit it when you can. If you have no edge, you can't trade for profit. If you know you have no edge, but you are trading for other reasons, you will lose.[3]

The players in markets who lose over the long run are generally commercial hedgers. The reason for this is that hedgers use the markets for risk insurance, and insurance premiums always cost money.[4] Of course, other speculators with bad strategy can provide winners with their gains too.

> Buying high and selling low, over the long run, keeps you opposite hedgers who eventually pay for the privilege of transferring their risk to the markets.[5]

As counterintuitive as it seems, if you buy higher highs and sell short lower lows, and you use solid money management to manage and exit trades, you can find a mathematical edge in the long run. This keeps you opposite hedgers as much as possible. It is not rocket science by any means, but it holds up over time very robustly.[6]

The market is brutal. Forget trying to be loved. Need a friend? Get a dog. If you are going to win, someone else will lose, either through their hedging or their bad strategy. Does survival of the fittest make you uneasy? Stay out of the zero-sum game.

> Someone's gotta lose for you to win.[7]

*All evolution in
thought and conduct
must at first appear as
heresy and misconduct.*[1]

Crash and Burn

The world changed in October 2008. Stock markets crashed. Millions lost their retirement money when their buy-and-hold strategies imploded. The Dow, S&P, and Nasdaq fell like stones. Most everyone has felt the ramifications: jobs lost, firms bankrupt, and universal fear still to this day causing daily heartburn.

No one made money during 2008. Everyone lost. Is that really true? No. There were trend following winners during October 2008, and they made fortunes ranging from +5 percent to +40 percent in that single month. How did they do it? First, let me state how they did *not* do it:

> **Market boom goes to market ka-boom!**

- Trend followers did *not* know stock markets would crash in October 2008.
- Trend followers did *not* make all of their money from shorting stocks in October 2008.

What did they do exactly? Trend followers made money in many different markets: oil, bonds, currencies, stocks, and commodities—via up and down trends going both *long* and *short*. Of course, there was zilch press coverage of their big wins. Academics and their peer-reviewed journals—nope—they were at the three-martini lunch too. Lack of public profile is nothing new—trend following anonymity goes back 50 years. (I probably have the most complete private trend following library available, but very little of it is online or at universities.)

The reason trend following performs so well when equity markets perform worst is straightforward: When an event happens, it reinforces a crisis mentality already in place, and trends drive toward a final conclusion—where the really big money is made as fear reaches a zenith, and markets go parabolic. This is the reason trend following rarely gets caught on the wrong side of an event (or crash)—there is almost always advanced warning for those who observe price action.[2]

Competing messages can make that simple wisdom difficult to accept. The magazine *Wired* recently described the issues:

Complexity researchers who study behavior of stock markets may have identified a signal that precedes crashes. They say the telltale sign is a measure of co-movement, or the likelihood of stocks to move in the same direction. When a market is healthy, co-movement is low. But in the months and years before a crash, co-movement seems to grow. "The financial crisis has shown that mainstream economic theories have limitations that need to be overcome," said Dirk Helbing of the Swiss Federal Institute of Technology, who specializes in modeling crowd behavior. "Economic systems have become much more complex, and complex systems have certain features—cascading effects, systemic shifts. This calls for new theoretical approaches."[3]

When will mainstream publications, the ones who love to reveal *new thinking*, learn that strategies that take advantage of crashes already exist? Surprise: trend following.

> Trends do not continue on to the Moon as per extrapolation lines neatly drawn with a ruler. They flatten, reverse, or crash.[4]

To do that means you must have a portfolio with enough exposure to diverse global markets to allow you to make the crazy money during the big events. And there will inevitably be more surprise events with headline-generating losers taking the perp walk in the press, with the winners going unknown.

That is a prediction worth betting on.

"Could you be on
a desert island and make
money trading?"
That is the question
to answer.[1]

Inefficient Markets

The hedge fund Long Term Capital Management (LTCM) went bust in 1998, and that event is more relevant today than ever. It laid the foundation for government induced bubble/bailout schemes still employed daily.

LTCM promised to use complex mathematical models to make investors wealthy beyond their wildest dreams. It attracted elite Wall Street investors and initially reaped fantastic profits with *secret* money-making strategies. Ultimately, its theories collided with reality.

To understand the LTCM debacle, it starts with two academic legends: Merton Miller and Eugene F. Fama who developed the Efficient-Markets Hypothesis. The premise of their hypothesis was that stock prices were always right so you could not divine the market's future direction. It assumed that everyone was rational.[2]

Miller and Fama believed that perfectly rational people would never pay more or less for a financial instrument than it was actually worth. A colleague, and fervent supporter of the Efficient-Markets Hypothesis, Myron Scholes was also certain that markets could not make mistakes. He and his associate, Robert Merton, saw the finance universe as tidy and predictable.

They assumed that the price of IBM would never go directly from 80 to 60 but would always stop at 79 3/4, 79 1/2, and 79 1/4 along the way.[3] LTCM's founders believed the market was a perfect normal distribution with no outliers, no fat tails, and no unexpected events.

Once Wall Street was convinced by LTCM that the markets were a nice, pleasant, orderly, and continuous normal distribution, with no risk, LTCM began using mammoth leverage for supposedly risk-free big returns. That is where problems started. They ignored the unexpected in their strategy. If a random bolt of lightning hits you when you are standing in the middle of a field, it might feel like a random event. But if your business is to stand in random fields during lightning storms, then you are clearly ignoring obvious and real risks.[4]

> **If a trader believes he's got magic over discipline, run for the hills, partner.**

Trend followers made a killing as LTCM went through the cheese grater. Returns for trend following traders in August and September of 1998 were almost like one continuous credit card swipe direct from LTCM. LTCM lost billions and top trend followers made billions.[5]

Yet it's worse than just one hedge fund blowing up and trend followers winning again. Eugene Fama's efficient market misstep has also given mutual funds the cover they needed to raise massive assets (and **milk** insane fees out of the average Joe).

For the last 30 years, there has been a sophisticated marketing campaign, boosted by an even more sophisticated political lobbying campaign, all designed to convince everyone attached to the *matrix* that they could do no better than guessing or throwing darts, so in turn just "invest all of your money in mutual funds and hold on for the long term" (long term is never usefully defined of course; it could be your death).

For a man who has the numbers against him, Fama remains defiant in the face of his intellectual defeat. Recently he was asked this question about technical trading (read: trend following): "Some researchers argue that a market-timing strategy based on buy/sell signals generated by a 50- or 200-day moving average offers a more appealing combination of risk and return than a buy-and-hold approach. What is your view?"

Fama responded: "An ancient tale with no empirical support." Clearly, Fama has no answer for the reality of trend following performance. He would rather commit Seppuku—a form of Japanese ritual suicide—than admit an error. He would rather die with honor than fall into the hands of superior market wisdom.[6]

> If you don't know who you are, the markets are an expensive place to find out.[8]

Having lived through the financial crisis of 2007–08, the man in the street knows markets are not efficient. But the Efficient-Market Hypothesis, like a Hollywood monster, has proved very hard to kill off.[7]

Fortunately for you, there is a way out. There is inspiration. The great trend followers are not academics, magicians, charlatans, or pedigreed investment bankers. They are self-starter entrepreneurs who, through concentration, drive, and fierce independent streaks, have cultivated that rare knowledge to mint money. Trend following proves daily that the Efficient-Markets Hypothesis has more in common with Scientology, versus any useful trading enlightenment. Understand the comparisons made herein. It's all part of you interpreting the puzzle.

Who's to blame?
Well certainly, there are those more
responsible than others,
and they will be held accountable,
but again, truth be told, if you're
looking for the guilty, you need only
look into a mirror.[1]

Benchmark

If you base your trading strategy on benchmark comparisons, it does not matter whether you are a brilliant trader. All your decisions are made with respect to what the averages are doing, so just sit back and take whatever the market gives you.

One of the main reasons trend following trading performs so well is because it has no quarterly performance constraints. What does that mean exactly? Both Wall Street and Main Street measure success on the artificial constraints of the calendar year.

An unnatural fascination with quarterly and yearly performance reporting implies you can predict the market or successfully shoot for profit targets. Quarters provide a comfortable structure for those who mistakenly believe they can demand nice, consistent profits in the time frame of their choosing. ("I want to make money in the third quarter.") This demand for consistency and predictability has led to a fruitless search for the trading Holy Grail.

Imagine you are playing American football. There are four quarters, and you have to score in each quarter to win. Imagine placing more importance on scoring in each quarter than winning the game. "I might score 28 points in any of the four quarters. I might score at any point in the game, but the object, at the end of the game is to win." If you score 28 points in the first quarter and no points in the next three quarters, and win, who cares when you scored?

Wall Street's misguided emphasis on quarterly performance puts more importance on scoring each quarter than it does on winning the game. Seriously, how many bad Star Trek jokes about Spock logic could be inserted to counter this craziness?

One big-name trader publicly lamented quarterly reporting comparing it to a necessary but incompetent baseball umpire: "If you don't have an umpire, you can wait for the fat pitch. The trouble with investing for other people…is that you do have an umpire—called quarterly performance."[2]

If so many market players know the umpire of quarterly performance is ridiculous, why do they stick with it? Wall Street has done it on purpose. The corporate quarterly earnings "seasons" are attempts to push up stocks by slicing and dicing statistics to portray companies in their best possible light.

Similarly, each time an administration changes the government, watch closely how the quarterly and monthly labor and GDP statistics change and are recalibrated to portray the incumbent political party in the best possible light.

Quarterly measure and benchmarks are not behind trend following fortunes. Trend following in its purest form is about absolute returns—making the most money possible while not tied to some random calendar date. I know this all might seem pedantic, but look at how much of our economy is tied to this backward way of thinking.

In a nation ruled by swine, all pigs are upwardly mobile and the rest of us are f***ed until we can put our acts together: not necessarily to win, but mainly to keep from losing completely. We owe that to ourselves and our crippled self-image as something better than a nation of panicked sheep.[3]

Life is tough.

Wear a cup.[1]

Haters

Big events allow huge money to change hands and that often brings public whinings and floggings. Many critics pose *meaning of life* questions when one group loses dramatically in public to another group. Their *caring* is heartfelt. They ask the virtuous questions:

1. What do these events tell us about our society?
2. Are these financial losses the dark side of all the benefits of financial derivatives?
3. Should we change the way we do things?
4. Should the society accept these financial losses as part of the "survival of the fittest" in the world of business?
5. Should legislation be used to avoid these events?[2]

These questions are designed to absolve the guilt of market losers for their bad strategy. A free market is no place for political excuses, social engineering, or more bailouts.

Consider fund manager Anthony Ward. He supposedly "cornered" the cocoa market. By one estimate, he bought enough to make five billion chocolate bars. Critics accused him of stockpiling cocoa to drive up prices so he could sell later at a profit. (Cocoa prices on the London market were at a 30-year high.)[3]

One bright trader tries to make a dollar in an open market, and rival traders complain that he is trying to make money? What are they trying to do? *Lose money?*

It gets worse. One reader recently asked about the *value*

> Price is the final arbiter of wisdom. To paraphrase *Bull Durham*, "Don't think, Meat, trade."[4]

trend following added, beyond the potential profit. That's a very odd question. What more value does he want? You trade, you make money, and that's it. Look at the case of John Paulson, the man who made a fortune betting against real estate.

A note posted about his success caught my eye: "Left unexamined is the uncomfortable moral dimension of Paulson's achievement. If he saw this coming, was it right for him to keep his own counsel, quietly trading while the financial system melted down? Do traders who figure out a way to profit from our misery deserve our contempt or our admiration, however grudging?"

Paulson deserves admiration. If you hate Paulson's success (and if/until it is proven he did it dishonorably), you have issues to work out with your shrink. The profit opportunity was there for all. He had the same information or less over banks, government, and bigger funds who lost big. He was making trades with the very banks that went bankrupt. Paulson chose to leave the crowd and bet with a novel strategy. Salute, not scorn.

> Improbable financial events, just like earthquakes, can't be predicted.

Blaming winners reminds me of the reaction after a meteorite hits Springfield in an episode of *The Simpsons*. Everyone screams: "Let's burn down the observatory so that never happens again!"

In the old U.S.S.R.

you waited all day for

"free" bread.

The Root of All Evil

Thanks to Facebook, generations are willing to share anything and everything.

However, many are still ambivalent about money. Some want more money, but feel guilty about openly admitting it. A few have lots and feel guilty for reasons that don't make sense. Many feel guilt if they did not come about it honestly (as they should) or at least in proportion to their labor to achieve it. Some dream of making a sex tape and building a reality TV empire. Fair enough. Yet take a moment to think through your motivations for trading. If you have any reason for trading except to make money, find something else to do and avoid the stress from the start.

There is nothing good or bad about money. Money is just a tool. Ayn Rand countered brilliantly the desire of some to classify money as *evil*: "You think that money is the root of all evil? Have you ever asked what is the root of money? Money is a tool of exchange, which can't exist unless there are goods produced and men able to produce them. Money is the material shape of the principle that men who wish to deal with one another must deal by trade and give value for value. Money is not the tool of the moochers, who claim your product by tears, or of the looters, who take it from you by force. Money is made possible by the men who produce. Is that what you consider evil?"[2]

> You don't own your possessions, your possessions own you.[1]

If all ethical people think money is bad, who's going to get the money?[3] That's my question. Here is a great example of money and emotions in full bloom. Years back, talk show king Phil Donahue was interviewing free-market economist Milton Friedman. He wanted to know if Friedman had ever had a moment of doubt about capitalism and whether he thought greed was really a good idea.

Friedman was quick in response: "Is there some society you know that doesn't run on greed? You think Russia doesn't run on greed? You think China doesn't run on greed? The world runs on individuals pursuing their separate interests. The great achievements of civilization have not come from government bureaus. Einstein didn't construct his theory under order from a bureaucrat. Henry Ford didn't revolutionize the automobile industry that way. The only cases in which the masses have escaped from the kind of grinding poverty you're talking about, the only cases in recorded history, are where they have had capitalism and largely free trade. If you want to know where the masses are worst off, it's exactly in the kinds of societies that depart from that."[4]

Donahue countered that capitalism doesn't reward virtue, but instead rewards the ability to manipulate the system. Friedman balked: "And what does reward virtue? You think the communist commissar rewards virtue? Do you think American presidents reward virtue? Do they choose their appointees on the basis of the virtue of the people appointed or on the basis of their political clout? Is it really true that political self-interest is nobler somehow than economic self-interest? Just tell me where in the world you find these angels who are going to organize society for us?"[5]

America has long seen certain contingents push the belief that there could be a government angel to let the proletariat have more money—with no effort.

Consider President Franklin Delano Roosevelt talking to America on January 11, 1944. He gave a caring government hug across the airwaves as he proposed what he called a second Bill of Rights—an economic Bill of Rights for all regardless of station, race, or creed that included

- The right to a useful and remunerative job in the industries or shops or farms or mines of the nation.
- The right to earn enough to provide adequate food and clothing and recreation.
- The right of every farmer to raise and sell his products at a return that will give him and his family a decent living.
- The right of every businessman, large and small, to trade in an atmosphere of freedom from unfair competition and domination by monopolies at home or abroad.
- The right of every family to a decent home.
- The right to adequate medical care and the opportunity to achieve and enjoy good health.
- The right to adequate protection from the economic fears of old age, sickness, accident, and unemployment.
- The right to a good education.[6]

What is left for us to accomplish if the government gives us all of that?

Come on. Let's face it head on. The market does not care about you or me. If you can accept that reality, then you can deal with it and trade it. You need to decide how much money you want over the course of a lifetime. You want a little? Or do you want a lot? Or are you satisfied believing empty investment promises made by suits in Washington D.C.? Regardless, you will get **exactly** what you want out of life through your actions.

It is the survival of the fittest. Eat dinner or be dinner.

There's no such thing as too high of a price or too low of a price.

Michael Covel extra article: http://mises.org/daily/3751.

*Ladies and gentlemen,
please take your seats
and fasten your brain.
We're entering clear-airhead
turbulence.*

Panicky Sheep

You see them. Maybe you are one. Some are so connected to their BlackBerry, they can't imagine it not being in their hand 24/7. Compulsive gaming. Second Life. Sparknotes. People are looking at screens, sometimes multiple screens. Some think teaching students to multitask is important for future jobs. Jobs doing what? Serving Ritalin with a splash of Patrón?

Attention deficit disorder is so pervasive, and so ubiquitous, that very few of us even see it as a major concern. People are supremely distracted, and that equals behaviors driven by the moment. Not behaviors purposeful and thought out.

> "Would you tell me, please, which way I ought to go from here?"
>
> "That depends a good deal on where you want to get to," said the Cat.
>
> "I don't much care where," said Alice.
>
> "Then it doesn't matter which way you go," said the Cat.[1]

While making a documentary film (brokemovie.com), one of the first places my crew visited was a sheep farm. Those animals were so scared to be separated from the group it is terribly hard to put their fear into words. Late in the day of the shoot, I got really close to the herd and tried to split them in half. They panicked to reform their group. They had to get back to one cohesive crowd. They made no sounds. Their faces were expressionless. They just moved their feet—fast.

Humans live to be part of a group too: The group offers safety, confirmation, and simplifies decision-making. Further, if something goes wrong, it is far more comforting to be with others than to be alone—the old saying, "misery loves company," rings true. However, the successful trader has to be willing to separate from the crowd—to be a contrarian—even though you might always have a strong emotional urge to stay with the group.

Additionally, human sheep behavior is shaped further by a proliferation of electronic goodies. Greed, hope, fear, denial, herd behavior, impulsiveness, and impatience are jacked up on gadget steroids. This is a recipe and foundation for manias and bubbles ad infinitum.[2]

Daniel Kahneman, the first psychologist to win the Nobel Prize in Economics, attributed market manias to investors' illusion of control, calling this illusion Prospect Theory. He wanted to know: How do people estimate odds and calculate risks? The short answer: Not smartly.[3]

People dislike losses so much that they will make nonstop irrational decisions in vain attempts to avoid the pain. This explains why traders, for example, sell winners too early but hold on to losers too long. It is human nature to take profit from a winner quickly on the assumption that it will not last for long, but stick with a loser in the hope it will bounce back.[4]

The typical trader acts on the "law of small numbers"—basing decisions on statistically insignificant examples. For instance, if you buy a fund that has beaten the market three years in a row, it is easy to become seduced that it's on a hot streak. It is hard for us to stop overgeneralizing. Limited empirical evidence is what drives life these days.[5]

> The storm starts when the drops start dropping. When the drops stop dropping then the storm starts stopping.

Any discussion of why traders are their own worst enemies starts with sunk costs. A *sunk cost* is a cost incurred you cannot retrieve. Although sunk costs should not affect your current decisions, people have a tough time leaving the past. Some will buy more of a losing stock just because of their initial decision to buy it. You can say proudly, "I bought on a discount!" or "I got it cheap." Of course, if that stock goes to zero, your theory dies.

Unfortunately, many are ambivalent to sunk costs. Intellectually, you might know that there is nothing you can do about money already spent, but emotionally dwelling on it is standard operating sheep deportment.

> Do you have a nerveless or nervous temperament? That is *your* choice.

An experiment with a $10 theater ticket illustrates this. One group of students was told to imagine they had arrived at a theater only to discover they had lost their ticket. Would they pay another $10 to buy another ticket? A second group was told to imagine that they were going to a play, but had not yet bought a ticket. When they arrived at the theater, they realized they lost a $10 bill. Would they still buy a ticket? In both cases, the students were presented with the same question: Would you spend $10 to see the play? Eighty-eight percent of the second group, which had lost the $10 bill, opted to buy the ticket. However, the first group, the ticket losers, focusing on sunk costs, asked the question differently: Am I willing to spend $20 to see a $10 play? Only 46 percent said yes.[6]

What are some additional behaviors that virtually guarantee losses in the markets?

- Lack of discipline: It takes an accumulation of knowledge and sharp focus to trade successfully. Many would rather listen to the advice of others. They just want to *believe*, like Fox Mulder.
- Impatience: Some have an insatiable need for action. The day trading adrenaline rush and the gamblers' high can have heroin-like addiction pull.
- No objectivity: Some are unable to disengage emotionally from the market. They create a virtual "lifelong" marriage to their trades. Divorce is not an option.
- Greed: A desire for quick profit blinds many from the diligent work needed to actually win in the long run.
- Refusal to accept truth: Some do not want to believe that the only knowable truth is *price action*. They feel more secure following cult leaders serving Kool-Aid.
- Impulsive behavior: Many jump into investments based on the morning paper or *Good Morning America*. Thinking that if you act quickly, somehow you will beat everybody else in the great race is a recipe for a messy failure.
- Inability to stay in the moment of *now*: To be a successful trader, you cannot spend your time thinking about how you are going to spend your profits. Trading because you have to have money is not workable.
- Stay open-minded: Come into the day knowing your future steps. Do not be stubborn when the market does not go your way. Cut your losses and follow your stinking trading plan.
- Avoid false parallels: Just because the market behaved one way in 1995, 2000, or 2008 does not mean a similar pattern today will give you the same result. A great example of this: *The Hindenburg Omen*. It is a technical analysis pattern that is said to portend a stock market crash. The problem: Sometimes it is right, sometimes not. You don't want to bet your life savings on a coin flip.

These behaviors all remind us that unlike in the animal world, where a threat passes quickly, humans live in constant stress. For 99 percent of animals, stress is about three minutes of screaming terror and the threat is over. We turn on the exact same stress response when pondering 30-year mortgages. What is quickly emerging as the biggest public-health problem everywhere? Depression.[7] You want to avoid that fate? Golf legend Jack Nicklaus is famous for saying: "Don't be too proud to take a lesson. I'm not. Learn the fundamentals of the game and stick to them. Band-Aid remedies never last."

The *fundamentals* of the trend following game include *behavior*.

People take comfort in doing what everyone else is doing, and if they are wrong, at least they are wrong with others.[8]

Doug: Either way, you gotta be super smart to count cards, buddy, okay?

Alan: Oh, really?

Doug: It's not easy.

Alan: Okay, well, maybe we should tell that to Rain Man, because he practically bankrupted a casino, and he was a ra-tard.

Stu: What?

Alan: He was a ra-tard.

Doug: Re-tard.[1]

IQ vs. EQ

Many believe academic intelligence is the direct path to reaping a fortune. Some literally tout their IQ—as if their IQ is money in their bank account. One longtime trend follower drilled that nonsensical stance: "I haven't seen much correlation between good trading and intelligence. Some outstanding traders are quite intelligent, but a few are not. Many outstandingly intelligent people are horrible traders. Average intelligence is enough. Beyond that, emotional makeup is more important."[2]

In an interview with one legendary trader, it struck me how he chose to begin. He opened by saying that when he was in kindergarten, he failed *blocks*. That humor is from a man worth north of 100 million. He is smart, but his point: IQ is no magic elixir.

> *Credentialism* is the short cut that relieves people from thinking.

Not only do people fall into the "IQ equals success" trap, they fall prey to thinking that a degree will take them to the top. That's 100% not true (see the book *Linchpin* for more). In fact, recent research takes my point further:

> [Look at] the livelihoods of plumbers and doctors. Yes, doctors have a bigger salary. But, doctors have to endure nearly a decade of expensive education before making any real salary, after which the doctor is hit by a very high progressive tax rate. Because of all the costs the doctor incurs, the taxes and the lost wages…plumbers make more, and have almost the same spending power over their lifetime as general practitioners.[3]

Consider those who pursue academic PhDs. A PhD is a specialist, not a generalist. In the real world, not the academic one, the generalist is today's winner. Not all PhDs are motivated entrepreneurial competitors capable of "killing it" (of course there are exceptions). A PhD, or any degree, does not protect you from failure. A degree says more than anything that we passed the test.

My comments are no knock against degree winners, but they are a reminder that it is you against the world. If you have a degree, any degree, that's awesome. I have three letters behind my name, but so what? Don't use the degree on the wall billboard, circa 1950s *Leave it to Beaver* America, to imply you are *special*. Those days are long gone…or maybe not!

The Associated Press recently ran with this frightening slug line:

NEW YORK—Today's college students are more narcissistic and self-centered than their predecessors, according to a comprehensive new study by five psychologists who worry that the trend could be harmful to personal relationships and American society. Stop endlessly repeating "You're special" and having children repeat that back. Kids are self-centered enough already.

I see those kids everyday—most are *adults*!

> I have been broke three or four times. But fortunately for me I'm not an MBA, so I didn't know I was broke.[4]

Some of the factors that will influence how well you do in life include self-awareness, self-discipline, intuition, empathy, and an ability to enter the *flow*. These traits are particularly useful for garnering profits from the markets. Yet many stay preoccupied on other facets of trading, even when leaving the *mental* part out is guaranteed long-term failure.[5]

This is not easy. Biological impulses are drivers of our emotions. There is no way to escape that fact, but you can learn to self-regulate your feelings and, in so doing, manage situations where emotions can interfere with sound decision-making—like in the markets. Self-regulation is the ongoing inner conversation that emotionally intelligent people engage in to not be a prisoner to their feelings.[6]

The ability to delay gratification, stifle impulsiveness, and shake off the inevitable setbacks and upsets is critical. Without emotional intelligence, you can have superior trend following training and systems, using an incisive and analytical mind with infinite creativity, and still fail.[7]

How can you start down that *right* path? The path to accepting the emotional part of your consciousness means focusing on improving your happiness:

- Do not equate happiness with money. You will acclimate quickly to shifts in income, but long-lasting benefits for all of us are negligible.
- Regular exercise generates energy and stimulates mind and body. Just do it.
- Having sex, preferably with someone you love, is often rated among the highest generators of happiness.
- Close relationships require serious work and effort, but pay huge rewards.

- Take time to appreciate the good things in life, a very simple habit that will help keep you from trouble.
- Seek work that engages your skills. It makes sense to work at something you enjoy.
- Sleep. Eight hours. Mandatory.
- Take control of your life and set achievable goals.

Follow all rules and please don't ask if these are actually relevant to trend following success.[8]

American Football coach
Jim Harbaugh would often ask his college
players to name the one thing needed
to make an NFL team.
The answers would come firing out:
"You have to be talented."
"You have to work hard."
No, Harbaugh would retort.
"A lot of guys are talented and work hard
and never make it.
The one thing you have to do to make
an NFL team is take another man's
job away from him.
And those men really like those jobs."[1]

Commitment

What does life-changing commitment involve? Most people want to be *right*. They get satisfaction in having other people know that they are right. They seemingly do not want success. They do not appear to want winning. They do not seem to care much about money. They simply want to be *right*.

Winners just want to win.

That means you commit to patience and faith in a trading system that is not structured on quarterly reporting or some other artificial measure of the masses (read: sheep). You work hard to gain experience and knowledge. You commit to thinking and planning for the long term. Don't worry too much about the dollar amount in your paycheck from the man. Do not live by the herd's standard of salary success—those usually suck.

Further, simply reading trading philosophies and rules alone will not make you *hungry*. If you do not want to win, if you do not have it in your makeup, or if you cannot figure out how to put it into your makeup, you will lose.

Commitment to trend following is just like the commitment needed to be a top athlete. If you want to be a fantastic baseball player, you go to the batting cages on Friday night while your buddies are partying. You never give up the focus. By the time you get to the big leagues, you have what you want. However, the only reason you reached that goal is because you made the commitment at the outset to be a winner. Everyone wants the big leagues and the big money, but are you committed to making it happen with relentless and spirited determination?

Many do not recognize that they have a choice:

- Do something new and do not run with the pack.
- Collaborate with meaningful people.
- Be guided by beauty. It is a beautiful thing to solve problems and do things right.
- Do not give up.
- Hope for some good luck.[2]

Wisdom If You Want to Live Big:

You have to wake up every day with a deep desire to be successful. You cannot just wake up and say, "Hey, I'm going to give a little bit of effort today and see what happens." What, are you going to say when you fail, "I tried" and complain to your wife or girlfriend if it does not work out.[3]

• • •

"You can do anything in life; you just can't do everything." That's what Bacon meant when he said, "A wife and children were hostages to fortune." If you put them first, you probably won't run the three-and-a-half-minute mile, make your first $10 million, write the great American novel, or go around the world on a motorcycle. Such goals take complete dedication.[4]

• • •

Those who dare not simply exist. They do not live.[5]

• • •

You are much better off going into the market on a shoestring feeling that you cannot afford to lose. I would rather bet on somebody starting out with a few thousand dollars than on somebody who came in with millions.[6]

• • •

Most little gambles are made without any thought and may certainly be trivial. "Do I tie my shoes?" Seems to offer no big risk, nor any big reward. While others, such as a wildly careening bus coming toward you could have a far greater impact. However, if deciding not to tie your shoes causes you to trip and fall down in the middle of the road and that careening bus comes ripping at you, well then, in hindsight the trivial has suddenly become paramount.[7]

• • •

Be a big thinker. Be on fire. Live your imagination. Bet the farm. Do not take no for an answer. Turn reality into fantasy. Live your life with purpose.[8]

• • •

Rich and powerful people are not notably talented, educated, charming, or good-looking. They became rich and powerful by wanting to be rich and powerful. Your vision of where or who you want to be is the greatest asset you have. Without a goal it is impossible to score.[9]

When you really believe
that trading is simply a
probability game, concepts
like right and wrong or
win and lose no longer have
the same significance.[1]

Decide Now

Even if you knew the results of 10,000 roulette spins, what materials the roulette wheel was made of, and whatever hundred other pieces of information you could dream up as possibly being useful, you still would not know what really mattered: where the ball will land next.[2]

Similarly, flip a coin 10,000 times. What are the odds it will land on heads on the 10,001st flip? The odds are exactly 50 percent. Do you actually need to flip the coin 10,000 times to prove those odds?

If you put trend following into a baseball analogy you would ask: Do you want to play ball or do you not want to play ball? The pitch is coming across the plate. Decide now whether you will swing the bat. When the pitch comes, if it is your pitch, swing the bat. You want to wait for more information before you swing? No time. In an uncertain world, if you wait until the data is clear or until the ball has crossed the plate, you will miss the pitch.

> Luck is largely responsible for my reputation for genius. I don't walk into the office in the morning and say, "Am I smart today?" I walk in and wonder, "Am I lucky today?"[3]

In almost every competitive field, it has often been assumed that the best decision makers have the time and ability to process vast amounts of information. However, that is not true—time is always scarce. The principle of a fast and frugal *heuristic* is about using the minimum amount of time, knowledge, and computation to make adaptive choices in real life.[4]

Smart decision makers have learned to use a single piece of information to make tough decisions.[5] If you reflect, consider your options and alternatives, or try to second-guess yourself, you might end up making the wrong decision or even the right decision, but only after taking perhaps too much valuable time to get there.

Consider the simple act of catching a baseball. (Yes, I played some baseball.) It may seem that you would have to solve complex differential equations in your heads to predict the trajectory of a ball to catch it. In reality, you simply use a heuristic. For example, when a ball comes in high, you fix-ate on the ball and start running to it. You ignore the ball's initial velocity, distance, and angle, and focus on one piece of information, the angle of your gaze needed to catch it.[6]

Think about the markets. You wake up and see a market move enough to cause you to take action. If your rule says buy at price level 20, you do it. If you want to win, you execute the entry signal as prescribed. What do you want? Do you want fantasy, fun, excitement, and a lottery-like existence? Or do you want to execute correctly and win as a trend following trader by mak-ing your buy and sell decisions based on a single piece of information...the simple recognition heuristic of price.

Do not believe in anything simply because you heard it. Do not believe in anything simply because it is rumored by many. Do not believe in anything simply because it is found written in your religious books. Do not believe in anything merely on the authority of your teachers and elders. Do not believe in traditions because they have been handed down for many generations. But after observation and analysis, when you find that anything agrees with reason and is conducive to the good and benefit of one and all, then accept it and live up to it.[7]

Our approach to markets is a
science. It is an unpublished
science, but it is a real one.
You would have thick leather-bound
volumes of papers on it if there were a
willingness to "open the kimono,"
as the horrible modern expression has it.
The process of trading our system is like
repeatedly drawing different colored balls
from the statistician's apocryphal bag.
As we draw out a ball it becomes part of
the track record, and we put it back in
the bag, but there is no guarantee that the
balls will come out in the same order
in the future.[1]

Science

"Do you have a clear sense of probabilities and payoffs?"

Did you answer "no?" If so, you need to figure it out, and fast.

For example, trader Jim Simons (arguably a *closeted* trend trader—he does not identify as one), worth about $8.5 billion, has said that the advantage scientists brought to the trading table was not their computing or math skills, but their ability to *think* scientifically. That means the scientific method is in play:

1. Define the question/theory.
2. Gather information and resources (observe).
3. Form hypothesis.
4. Perform experiment and collect data.
5. Analyze data.
6. Interpret data and draw conclusions that serve as a starting point for new hypothesis.
7. Publish results.
8. Retest (frequently done by other scientists).

> Understanding trend trading is like crime scene investigation (CSI).

Sometimes scientists employed by trend trading firms are astrophysicists. Why? Astrophysics is an observational science. You have to learn by studying what is there. You cannot create an experimental solar system in the laboratory.[2]

For example, take a stock, multiply the number of firm employees by the sales, then divide by the dividend and subtract the CEO's age and you get a number. But so what? Just because you can compute that number does not make that number useful for anything. Scientific thinking immediately sees the logical errors.[3]

Being wrong is part of the trend following life. Many just cannot wrap their head around that.[4] Bottom line, there are scientifically established principles of market behavior that you can observe and use for profit. As Ripley said, "Believe it, or not!"

> Trend followers essentially operate scientific research labs. Their research materials are financial data.
> The financial markets are their laboratory.

Anton Chigurh: What's the most you ever lost on a coin toss?

Gas Station Owner: Sir?

Anton Chigurh: The most. You ever lost. On a coin toss.

Gas Station Owner: I don't know. I couldn't say.

[Chigurh flips a quarter from the change on the counter and covers it with his hand.]

Anton Chigurh: Call it.

Gas Station Owner: Call it?

Anton Chigurh: Yes.

Gas Station Owner: For what?

Anton Chigurh: Just call it.

Gas Station Owner: Well, need to know what we're calling it for here.

Anton Chigurh: You need to call it. I can't call it for you. It wouldn't be fair.

Gas Station Owner: I didn't put nothin' up.

Anton Chigurh: Yes, you did. You've been putting it up your whole life; you just didn't know it.[1]

Statistical Thinking

Trend following is about non-normality of market returns. You will never have, nor will you ever, produce returns that exhibit a normal distribution. You will never produce the mythologically consistent returns that many believe to exist.

When trend followers hit home runs from the likes of Barings Bank, Long-Term Capital Management, and the 2008 market crash, they are targeting unknowable extreme occurrences that happen to occur with a probability greater than expected.

> The Sharpe ratio is oversold. It can give a false sense of precision and lead people to make predictions unwisely.[2]

Those occurrences are *fat tails*—in statistician speak. Trend following's nature of riding a trend to the end when it *bends*, and then cutting losses very fast, puts you in a position to benefit when the next unexpected flood rolls in.

Trend following's *alpha* comes from letting winners run on the right-hand side of a fat tail and cutting losses short on the left-hand side. Eliminating losing positions and holding onto profitable positions puts you in the big game hunt for positive outliers.[3] A normal distribution is simply worse than useless as a risk management tool.[4]

> Trend followers exhibit a positive skew return profile.

Here is a great example of very *predictable* numbers: Professional baseball player Albert Pujols' career batting statistics:[5]

Year	G	AB	R	H	2B	HR	RBI	BB	SO	BA	SLG
2001	161	590	112	194	47	37	130	69	93	.329	.610
2002	157	590	118	185	40	34	127	72	69	.314	.561
2003	157	591	137	212	51	43	124	79	65	.359	.667
2004	154	592	133	196	51	46	123	84	52	.331	.657
2005	161	591	129	195	38	41	117	97	65	.330	.609
2006	143	535	119	177	33	49	137	92	50	.331	.671
2007	158	565	99	185	38	32	103	99	58	.327	.568
2008	148	524	100	187	44	37	116	104	54	.357	.653
2009	160	568	124	186	45	47	135	115	64	.327	.658
2010	159	587	115	183	39	42	118	103	76	.312	.596
Game avg.	162	596	123	198	44	42	128	95	67	.331	.624

Look back at the chapter "Show Me the Money." Trend following returns don't come close to exhibiting the consistency of Pujols' career statistics. You won't have trend following batting statistics that ever match Pujols' year in year out steadiness, but that is ok.

I acknowledge that consistency is a temptress—even for the highly educated and affluent. An associate of mine, an accomplished businessman, and I recently had lunch. He knew some about my career, but not much. During our conversation he mentioned that he was recently caught up in a very well-known hedge fund scam (not Madoff). I asked him quickly, before he could explain much, if his returns were positive every month. He replied, "Every month."

Later, I Googled him and found out that he had lost several million. However, thinking in terms of statistics is more than just measuring where on the bell curve trend traders find their inconsistent profits. For example, I want you to look at statistics from an alternative perspective.

Imagine there are two hospitals. In the first, 120 babies are born every day. In the second, 12 babies are born every day. On average, the ratio of boys to girls is 50/50. On a given day, in one of the two hospitals, twice as many girls are born as boys. Which hospital was it more likely to happen in? The likelihood is higher in the smaller hospital. Why? Because the probability of a random deviation from the population mean decreases with an increase in sample size.[6]

Take two traders who win 40 percent of the time with their winners being three times as large as their losers. One has a history of 1,000 trades and the other has a history of 10 trades. Who has a better chance in the next 10 trades to have only 10 percent of their total trades end up winners instead of the typical 40 percent? The one with the 10-trade history has the better chance. Why? The more trades in a history, the greater the probability of averages holding true. The fewer trades, the greater the probability of moving away from the average.

Consider a friend who receives a stock tip, makes some quick money, and tells everyone about it. There is a big problem with this scenario. His population of winning tips is extremely small—one to be exact. That's statistically insignificant. He could just as easily follow his next hot tip and lose all of his money. One tip means nothing. The sample is essentially anecdotal evidence.

Thinking in terms of statistics is everywhere if you are observant. During a *Monday Night Football* game, one of the announcers, Ron Jaworski, put *numbers* and *odds* in perspective for playing the game of football: "Play calling is about probability, not certainty."

It is the same in trend following trading.

All else being equal, you want
strategies with the most positive
skew and the most negative
excess kurtosis. These would
be strategies with the fewest
occurrences of large
negative returns.[7]

Knowing others
is wisdom;
Knowing self is
enlightenment.
Mastering others
requires force;
Mastering self
needs strength.[1]

Aha!

Finding the truth takes time, energy, and many Aha! moments. Figuring *it* out is very similar to taking a jolt of electricity to the brain (not that I have done that exactly!).

One of those awakenings for me occurred upon learning about the existence of a documentary from the late 1980s that profiled trader Paul Tudor Jones. Jones is now worth $3.3 billion—so evidence of his early trading days was welcomed.[2]

My intuition said that this out-of-circulation documentary was going to deliver the unexpected, but it was extremely tough to locate. Amazon, eBay, and most other obvious venues were dead ends. When I finally found it through 'channels,' my gut was dead on.

The March 1987 documentary *Trader* was made when Jones was 32 years old with just 22 employees in his firm. Today, his firm has 300 employees and more than $10 billion under management. The documentary was all raw passsion. Jones and Peter Borish, his second in command at the time, were in the middle of a game with one simple goal: Get very rich. Borish knew there were no shortcuts: "I am graded instantly through the harshest teacher in the world—the market. There is no curve. I can't say, 'Boy, I was out late last night and everybody else in the class was at a pep rally for the football game and I only got a 70, but that was the highest in the class, so I still got an A.' It doesn't work that way in the market."[3]

Jones was living that nonexistent grade curve. In one scene at his Chesapeake Bay home, you could hear *it* in his voice as he described playing at the highest level: "Whether you are making 100% rate of return on $10,000 or $100,000,000, it doesn't make any difference. Right? If you complete 78 percent of your passes, it would be nice to be in the NFL. [But] if you are in college, high school, or elementary school, I am sure the thrill [of winning] is just as great."[4]

Later in the film, Jones reflects about his first boss, a famed cotton speculator named Eli Tullis: "The first year I did nothing but get his coffee. I was learning by osmosis. I was a glorified secretary, which is fine because I was soaking in everything, every move that he made and every step that he took."[5]

Jones was especially fond of one memorable experience with Tullis: "He sat there right in the middle of getting absolutely decimated across the board in these commodities with the most beautiful smile, the most incredibly elegant poise and stylish composure and just had a wonderful little chat with me for 45 minutes to an hour. I was just overwhelmed that anyone could be that strong."[6]

> Numbers don't lie.
> You are either in
> the black or
> you are not.

Tullis's poise under pressure changed Jones's perspective. It both inspired and taught him a priceless lesson. If you want to end up with a nonaverage net worth, a "learn from someone else" attitude is paramount. Putting your ego aside and admitting that you don't know it all isn't easy, but it is the mindset of true winners.

Dare to be rare.

The best inheritance a person can give to his children is a few minutes of his time each day.[1]

Hero Worship

I could not write this book without chapters outlining what trend following acceptance is up against. In the world of financial media—it is a full court press for your attention (read: your dollars). Yet it always strikes me very odd to see people worshipping random financial dogma or slick talking market gurus. Thinking about that brought back a memory from the now classic animated TV series *King of the Hill*, especially since I know of *names* in the financial world just like this story (drugs and all).

In one episode, a washed-up former Dallas Cowboys football player moves into Hank Hill's neighborhood. This former Cowboy was never very good during his career, but to weekend warriors like Hank and his buddies, it did not matter in the least. He was a former pro football player—he was a god to be worshipped. That is until they found out the real story of Big Willie:

> **Big Willie**: Hey, you guys wanna see some stuff from my career? It's the football from that kick I blocked. Oh, and here's a picture from that kick I blocked... and that's how I blocked that kick.
>
> **Hank**: That story gets better every time you tell it.
>
> But later, as Hank's son Bobby notes, Big Willie is not that impressive a football legend.
>
> **Bobby**: You know, for a guy who was a pro athlete, Willie's drunk a lot.[2]

Many see market gurus as religious prophets. When TV zombies say it's time to buy Google or dump Las Vegas Sands, many follow random advice blindly—mostly because of the name fame factor. Do you actually know anything *real* about these people? Or could they just be cartoons like Big Willie? If fame is a factor in your market choices—honk the horn and yell, "Booyah!"

So why do people listen to talking heads making predictions all day long? Are they thinking, "Maybe he will help me make millions in the stock market?" Or is it, "Maybe he's right in his Google timing, and I can make a killing right now?" Or is it really, "He's on TV; he has to be right!"

Think of it this way: A guru comes on and says buy Gold. Isn't he saying that to the whole world? Worse yet, if you allow yourself to buy on a guru tip, does he call you up when it's time to sell? Or are you just assuming when he says *buy*, Gold will go up forever and you'll never need to sell?

If you hear talk about geometry, astrology, or market turning points—reach for your wallet— you are about to be ripped off. If there is talk of cycle tops and bottoms, a scam is a brewin'.

There is a room on Wall Street that has a big white board. On the left side of the board is a list of reasons why the market went up today. On the right side there is a list of reasons why the market went down today. After the close, the experts go into the room and pick off a reason for what happened. After all, investors are always looking for the reasons why the market goes up or goes down. Any reason will do.[1]

Buy and Hope

Cosmetic and financial services are strikingly similar. They both sell *hope*. For instance, after the stock market bubble burst in spring 2000 and after the crash of October 2008, the concept of buy and hold as a strategy should have died a stake-to-the-heart death. Despite everything that should have been learned, most still follow this strategy.

Stay the course. Buy the dips. Never surrender.... Buy and hold mantras are junk science because you never answer the basic questions: "Buy how much of what?" "Buy at what price?" "Hold for how long?"

Consider the Nasdaq market crash of 1973–1974. The Nasdaq reached its high peak in December 1972. It then dropped by nearly 60 percent, hitting rock bottom in September 1974. The Nasdaq did not break free of the 1973–1974 bear market until April 1980. Buy and hold did **nothing** from December 1972 through March 1980. Your golden years happened during the 1970s—tough luck. You would have made more money during this period in a 3-percent savings account. Of course, history repeated itself with the more recent 70+ percent drop in the Nasdaq from 2000–2009.

The buy and hold investor has been led to believe, by an industry with a powerful conflict of interest, that if you have tremendous patience and discipline and stick with it, you will make money. But you need to understand that you can go ten, and even twenty years, making no return at all, or even lose huge.

> Even a dead cat will bounce if you drop it from high enough.

To compound problems even more, buy and holders often fall prey to a form of market revenge. You bought, then you lost, and now you want your money back. You think, "I lost my money in MSFT, and I'm going to make my money back in MSFT come hell or high water. I will just hold on!" Not wise.

The examples do not stop. The Japanese Nikkei 225 stock index reached nearly 40,000 in 1989. Now, 22 years later, it is around 10,000. Do you think the Japanese still believe in buy and hold?

Dow Jones Industrial Average (DJIA): 10,006 (March 1999) 14,164 (October 2007) 12,339 (February 2011)

Nasdaq Composite: 5048 (March 2000) 2789 (February 2011)

Nikkei 225 (Japan): 38,915 (Dec 1989) 10,600 (February 2011)

Buy and hold as a strategy only works for those who live forever. It also works for those who gravitate toward magical thinking and/or pixie dust. However, mutual funds still make a fortune selling you the dream:

Chart 9   Mutual Funds with Largest Fees

	10-Year Period	$21.40 Billion Total Fees Earned
Fidelity Magellan	99-08	$3.70B
Fidelity Contrafund	98-07	$3.00B
American Century Ultra	99-08	$2.30B
PIMCO Total Return	99-08	$3.00B
American Funds Inv Co Amer	98-07	$1.54B
Fidelity Growth & Income	99-08	$1.56B
American Funds Growth Fnd Amer	99-08	$2.10B
Fidelity Low-Priced Stock Fund	99-08	$1.66B
American Funds Europacific	98-07	$1.74B
Fidelity Dividend Growth	99-08	$0.80B

$21 billion in fees have been paid to mutual funds for no performance over the last ten years. Mutual funds are just big skimming operations. They skim a little off of everyone, and, before you know it, the head of Fidelity is worth $11 billion. Consider sobering statistics:

- The typical American household has net financial assets of $1,000.
- In 2016, Social Security benefits will exceed tax collections.
- At their peak, 46 percent of working Americans were covered by a pension plan. By 2005, it had declined to 17 percent.
- The Fed has reduced interest rates to 0—killing everyone with a savings or money market account.
- The Dow closed at 381.17 on September 3, 1929. The Dow closed above 381 on 11/23/1954—25 years after the 1929 high.[2]

Those numbers are not pretty. That said, investors have short and selective memories. If the market advances from a low point to any significant degree upward, buy and hold *feels* comfortable again. It can feel like market bubbles are a thing of the past—especially when so many talking heads are preaching recovery.

No one knows if there is a current bubble in stocks, but it is amazing that some people think they know. I had a conversation with a friend recently. He mentioned that real estate in Southern California was stabilizing (forget that debate for a moment), and then the conversation of *bubbles* came up. He quickly announced that we were not in a stock market bubble. I was amazed at his confidence. Has there ever been a time when the majority knew they were in the middle of a bubble? Bubbles are never clear until the dust settles.

One critic proffered: "Momentum works about 80 percent of the time."[3] Where does that statistic come from? How does one define "momentum"? What happens the other 20 percent of the time? Do you go bankrupt? Do you lose half your money? How do you define "of the time"? Do you make money eight out of ten years? Months? Weeks? The fact that a critic starts with a fabricated statistic should ring alarm bells immediately.

You got to know when
to hold 'em, know when to fold 'em,
know when to walk away
and know when to run.
You never count your money
when you're sittin' at the table.
There'll be time enough
for countin' when the
dealing's done.[1]

Convert

Over the years, my firm's trend following research work has put me in contact with thousands of investors and traders spread across more than 100 countries. That was never expected with the simple launch of a five-page web site in late 1996 titled TurtleTrader.com. Back then I paid a 22-year old programmer $4,000 for that bit of web design. He quickly disappeared back to Russia, and I became a self-taught HTML coder.

Today, out of that humble beginning, there is no one type of person who reaches out for trend trading insight. Readers and clients include men and women, young and old, from college students to billion-dollar hedge funds. My sites have become a central clearing for all that is systematic trend following trading.

One of the most interesting aspects of spreading this gospel is *conversion*. People who once viewed trading one way, but who were influenced to change via my work. An example? A new client signed on recently. He has a very popular national radio show and has been working with private clients for decades. His specialty? Putting his clients' money to work using fundamental analysis. How much trend trading experience did he have prior to my books? None that I am aware. My research firm helped him to move in the right direction, but that was not what especially struck me in this case.

He was very open in telling me why he became a client. There was one basic reason: After the market bottomed in Spring 2009, he saw no fundamental reason for equity markets to trend up, but they did. He decided at that moment, and in the context of seeing my books, that he needed new tools to deal with that clear discrepancy as soon as possible.

Our conversation and exchanges were inspiring. After decades of providing a service to his clients, he knew something was wrong. He understood that he had to make an adjustment in his business. Not many people do that. Many are like the arrogant professors at the University of Chicago believing markets are efficient, people are rational, and it's my way or the highway. Don't be like the professors. Be a sponge. Be open to the *new*.

> No one understands the digits scrolling by on the screen. It's noise.[2]

First principles, Clarice:
Read Marcus Aurelius.
Of each particular thing ask,
"What is it in itself?
What is its nature?"[1]

Oracle of Omaha

Warren Buffett has achieved his Holy Grail, and his success is severely saluted. But, can you achieve what he has done? Doubtful. He is the unobtainable exception to every rule.

Buffett is complex with a complex firm. He has been positioned as the buy and hold/value guy and has not done much to counter that view, but it is dead wrong. Buffett has traded serious size in currencies. Many times he has bet against the dollar. There is nothing wrong with that, but the thousands who attend his annual shareholder meetings do not know that, that is part of the *real* legend.

Buffett has also traded derivatives, but at one time he was once squarely against derivatives: "We have more money than ideas...one place the money certainly won't go is to derivatives. There's no place with as much potential for phony numbers as derivatives."[2]

His billionaire vice chairman, Charlie Munger, added: "To say that derivative accounting is a sewer is an insult to sewage."[3] Shortly after those statements, Buffet's firm sold $400 million of a new type of derivative security in a private placement to qualified institutional investors.[4]

To confound even more, a year later Buffett declared: "Derivatives are financial weapons of mass destruction, carrying dangers, while now latent, [but] potentially lethal. We view them as time bombs, both for the parties that deal in them and the economic system."[5]

Buffett's legend of *buy and hold* or *value* as his get-rich strategy has permeated public consciousness thoroughly for decades. Dozens of books spin the yarn. Yet when he launches a new derivatives strategy against his legend, either no one notices or those who do notice refuse to criticize. (That might hurt business, after all.)

A few years back, I sat down with a trend following trader. He has a 20-year plus track record making on average more than 20 percent a year. The topic of Warren Buffett came up during our discussion. While he was very respectful of Buffett, he was bewildered how some could call his trend following trading *luck*, but those same people could see Buffett as *skill*.

This same trader pointed out the thousands of trades he has made. He noted that his trend trading peers also had thousands of trades over decades. He saw it more logical to make an argument for Buffett's success as luck given the relatively few trades that made him so wealthy: Coke, Gillette, American Express, Goldman Sachs, and Wells Fargo to name a few.

In addition to the billions in options he wrote (more derivatives), Buffett's own portfolio and insurance business were arguably at the heart of the Great Recession. It may be a stretch to say that the solvency of Berkshire was at risk in the fall of 2008, but just imagine how things would have unfolded if Goldman Sachs had failed. The dominoes in Buffett's portfolio and behind Berkshire would have tumbled quickly.[6]

A few years later, in 2011, Buffett was in India warning investors to avoid "long-term fixed-dollar investments" such as 10-year U.S. Treasury bonds. He worried that government actions were combining to dilute the value of the dollar. Buffett warned: "If you ask me, if the U.S. Dollar is going to hold its purchasing power fully at the level of 2011, 5 years, 10 years, or 20 years from now, I would tell you it will not." Does that mean Buffett has been selling bonds? You bet. Amazingly, government actions he now critiques are the very ones that saved him.[7]

However, Buffett sees it differently. He reflected on the chaotic times since 2008: "[My techniques] are not new lessons. Never owe any money you can't pay tomorrow morning. Never let the markets dictate your actions. Always be in a position to play your own game. Never take on more risks than you can handle. But all of those were old lessons, unfortunately. Even though I didn't see it coming, those lessons which are timeless allowed us to in effect profit from it rather than suffer from it. Good businesses, good management, plenty of liquidity, always having a loaded gun; if you play by those principles, you will do fine no matter what happens. And you don't ever know what's going to happen."[8]

It's almost as if Buffett has become Jason Bourne—an amnesiac on the loose—without memory of how history has *really* unfolded. Add in his Goldman Sachs association and the David Sokol situation, a top executive of his who resigned under odd circumstances resembling insider trading, and in total over the last decade Buffett as the avuncular straight talker has become harder and harder to accept at face value. Long-time fund manager Michael Steinhardt was harsher: "[Buffett's] reality is that he is the greatest PR person of recent times. And he has managed to achieve a snow job that has conned virtually everyone in the press to my knowledge...and [it] is remarkable that he continues to do it."[9]

As someone who grew up in the Washington D.C. area, I watched politicians use and/or abuse the system to their own economic advantage on such

Don't drink the Kool-Aid.

a regular basis that it was no longer considered unethical. In the fall of 2008, Buffet received political favors and influenced government in ways that no trend following trader ever could. It was wrong. Buying into the Buffet legend is not part of my ethos.

A good friend of mine was once employed as a reporter by the largest commodity news service at the time. One day his major story was about Sugar and what it was going to do. After I read his piece, I asked: "Gary, how do you know all of this?" I will never forget his answer. He said: "I made it up."[1]

A Seinfeld Moment

The line between entertainment and today's financial journalism is very murky. First, consider an instantly recognizable passage for many comedy fans:

NBC Executive: I just wanted to let you know that we've been discussing you at some of our meetings and we'd be very interested in doing something.

Jerry: Really? Wow.

NBC Executive: If you have any idea for a TV show for yourself, well, we'd just love to talk about it.

Jerry: I'd be very interested in something like that.

NBC Executive: Well, why don't you give us a call and maybe we can develop a series.

Jerry: Okay. Great. Thanks.

George returns.

George: What was that all about?

Jerry: They said they were interested in me.

George: For what?

Jerry: A TV show.

George: Your own show?

Later Jerry and George are talking.

Jerry: Well, what's our new show idea going to be about?

George: It's about *nothing*.

Jerry: No story?

George: No, forget the story.

Jerry: You've got to have a story.

A little later.

Jerry: And it's about nothing?

George: Absolutely nothing.

Jerry: So you're saying, I go in to NBC, and tell them I got this idea for a show about nothing?

> CNBC is a network for those who are wealthy and those who want to be wealthy, and that's what we stay focused on every day.[2]

CNBC once invited me to their offices. They paid my travel. I had no specific knowledge of what they wanted, but the meeting was with producer Susan Krakower who had invented Jim Cramer's show. It was assumed that they were looking for new content. Once there, the meeting was in a small windowless New Jersey office with Krakower and her two lieutenants. It was like when Jerry and George went to meet with NBC. A Jim Cramer poster hung behind her.

Krakower sat in front of me behind a large desk and her two lieutenants flanked me on either side. It was triangulation so to speak. They peppered me with small talk questions, yet seemed to have no clue about my writings, research, or thinking. They had not read my books. They only had a picture of me that I had not seen before (something you might imagine an actor brings to a Hollywood casting call). *This* was the epicenter of CNBC's content development: A glossy headshot.

Krakower asked me to hypothetically program ten hours of airtime for CNBC. My idea for new programming was blunt: trend following, not more stories. My ability to play the game was not very good, and it was easy to see that candor was taken as an insult. The conversation bounced around for 30 minutes and—surprise, surprise—there was no further dialogue.

Walking through the halls of CNBC's studios that day reminded me of *The Truman Show*: a constructed reality, a staged, scripted TV show. Except instead of it being one person (Jim Carrey's character in *The Truman Show*) who does not know reality is fake, CNBC's reality plays to a worldwide audience daily, week after week and year after year. Views like that make me a persona non grata with some.

Once after speaking to an audience of nearly 1,000 in Brazil, and after the audience had just listened to me proselytize (come on, I got to play the title of this book up some!) about the negatives of media and press, the barbed wire question was thrown to rip me a new one:

"How are you different than Jim Cramer?"

Now that question came after an hour of talking about trend following in depth in the context of the 2008 market crash as trend followers cleaned up. But still, it was a great question to explain further. It comes down to fundamentals versus trend following. If you watch Cramer, you always have to tune in to stay current—that is the hook. That is not the trend following process. It is not my process. Once you know the trend trading *way*, you do not need anyone to hold your hand to cross the street. That's a big difference. Although, teaching as many people as possible is my goal, and capitalism courses through my veins, comparisons to Cramer do not equate.

My logic does not win everyone over. One reader complained: "You trash CNBC and other people, but they provide very good information if you know how to use it, and you shouldn't just trash everybody's point of view because there are a lot of smarter people than you who have a better opinion."

Punch harder *please*. Really get some shoulder into it if you are going to swing at me.

Let Federal government and mass media do what they do, which is to spend a ridiculous amount of time and energy attempting to justify their respective existence by providing information for the consumption of the knowledge-hungry masses. If one wishes to be wise one will acknowledge one's own ignorance, observe the herd from a distance, and perhaps shrug in amusement.[3]

The illiterate of the 21st century will not be those who cannot read and write, but those who cannot learn, unlearn, and relearn.[1]

Snow Job

After a presentation at the Traders Expo in Las Vegas, an investor approached me. He wanted to explain his belief that he could trade for profit based on his *gut* feel, using his intuition as his sole decision-making criteria. I immediately envisioned him sitting in his big easy chair staring into space deciding how his tummy felt. He mentioned a recent book that touted his belief, but otherwise he had no objective proof.

I said, "Please provide one legitimate performance record based on your type of decision-making? Just one will do." Spoiler alert: There is not one.

That does not stop the prophets though. Consider an end-of-the-world announcement put out November 10, 2010, by one guru:

> It used to be that someone could declare a positive return was their brilliance, rather than just the general rise of the broad market. Now you can tell the truth.

"This is one of those intuitions… We might even see a test of the post-crash lows of [S&P] 670 again before the market comes back. If any of you have a lot of money in the stock market, I'd suggest that now is a very good time to go to cash. 100% cash. If I were you I'd sell everything in my 401K etc. Sell mutual funds, individual stocks etc. The market is ripe for a correction and it could get ugly again. My intuition tells me that it could get worse than we've seen in recent memory. I don't generally make predictions and this isn't a prediction exactly as the price could certainly go higher."

It is the end of the world, but markets *could* go higher. Bottom line, flipping coins is not how people accumulate wealth. A month later, this same individual was asked about his prediction not working. He tried to save face:

"I think the markets are in for another series of problems, which will manifest sometime in the next week to five years, but the market action is neutral at this exact moment."

Next week to five years. That's his call?

Bullsh** just baffles brains. When you talk bullsh**, it's like you've thrown a baseball at someone. It is up to them to consider what you've said; i.e. to catch the ball. It is up to them to understand or respond. If your words consist of big meaningless words, which take people time to understand, then you've achieved your goal. Most do not want to appear foolish and will happily nod and agree just so it appears that they've understood to avoid any embarrassment (tip to madbot.org).

It gets more entertaining. Peter Popoff is an odd-looking fellow who I first saw while flipping channels. He is a German televangelist who preaches money to primarily African-American audiences in the American South. His videos are outrageous—lots of hands on the foreheads and supposed miracles of debt relief along with instant riches in the form of checks that just arrive in the mail.

Popoff and his brethren, because there is more than one that's for sure, are selling Jesus-based get-rich-quick and get-out-of-debt schemes to thousands. It's also the mainstream televangelists like Pat Robertson. He announced that "the Lord" had told him that there was going to be a major stock market crash in 2009 or 2010—a prediction that did not pan out.

It does not stop with preachers. Even the big-name celebrities are in on moving sheep from point A to point B:

> H & H Imports Inc. surged higher after rapper 50 Cent told his fans on Twitter to buy the stock that sells his new sunglasses: "HNHI is the stock symbol for TVG sleek by 50 is one of the 15 products this year. If you get in technically I work for you. BIG MONEY. Ok ok ok my friends just told me stop tweeting about HNHI so we can get all the money. Hahaha check it out its[sic] the real deal. HNHI is the stock symbol for TVG there[sic] launching 15 different products. They are no joke get in now."

It's not just the low-rent characters pushing you in the wrong direction, the so-called reputable sources push all of the wrong data at investors in a nonstop stream of consciousness. These *top* headlines were pulled from Fool.com:

- 3 Small Caps With Dividend Potential
- Where You'll Make Money in Housing
- 7 Guru Picks You Should Be Watching

- Are Interest Rate Hikes Imminent?
- 4 Dividend Stocks Showing You the Money
- 3 Favorite Stocks of the Wealthy
- 7 Reasons Not to Worry This Week
- 5 of Last Week's Biggest Winners
- 5 of Last Week's Biggest Losers

> If someone tells me they can predict the market, I ask one question: "What is it going to do tomorrow?"[2]

Once you become a trend follower, points like those will illicit an occasional soft smile from you, but you will never click again as you will *know* there is no "there there" behind the link, so to speak.

People so want to believe that there is a crystal ball reader who can solve life's problems. Believing helps many find meaning—in a world where meaning is often not to be found. Bottom line, cutting through garbage is not easy, especially when some prophets have famous resumes.

They believe [fill in the blank] because he screams at them with certainty and reduces all the complexities of a market into a cartoon bull or bear.

Twit Me a River

Twitter, chat rooms, message boards, e-mails from guys selling get rich fast—the desire to convince someone else of *something*—never ends. Twitter, however, is the one social media app that fascinates me. It is very cool conceptually. What a great way to reach people, to get a message out, and quick.

However, how can millions of tipsters and tweets bring actionable and credible advice on making money to you on a daily basis? They can't. It's too much information. It's not the most important information, either (remember *price?*). One inventive fellow, attempting to base his hedge fund around *tweets*, tossed this gem out:

> "If you can do this it gives you a massive edge on the market as you know the *mood*." The principle lies in analyzing the 120 million tweets, which are posted daily by the 180 million-strong Twitter members and looking for mood states. Using an algorithm which works in real time, it divides the information into six mood states—anxious, calm, and sad for example—giving them an overall reflection of how the world is feeling.[1]

Of course, this type of silly talk is not new. People have been leading and misleading each other since the dawn of time. You jump into that game, you get what you get, win or lose.

The government, not surprisingly due to their infinite *caring*, always want to help those who lose, even if they lose fairly due to

> One Internet charlatan promotes that he was nominated for a Nobel Prize. Never mind that there is no proof; hucksters will say anything.

their own choice or ignorance. How did the government recently try to fix the problem of losing? The SEC actually supported a new and improved ban of the spreading of false and misleading information about companies. Former SEC Chairman Christopher Cox said he wanted to ensure that investors could continue to get reliable, accurate information about public companies in the marketplace.

Nonsense. That protection already exists—it is called the **market price**. You cannot fake that.

I am not entirely certain how *misleading* can be clearly defined. But, suppose some knucklehead wants to spin misleading information on a chat board. And, then an even bigger knucklehead chooses to believe this information and act on it. That is a marriage made in heaven, not an opportunity for the federal government to step in and create more jobs—or what they call regulation.

In chat rooms, anonymity fuels a liar's sense of invincibility, and his statements are often so bold and outrageous it's amazing anyone takes it seriously. Yet there is no shortage of individuals ready to look for new confidants among the shadowy charlatans of the Internet.[2]

**We doin' big pimpin,
spendin' cheese.**[1]

Goldline

You have surely heard the Goldline.com commercials on TV and radio (or similar gold hype). They will sell you gold because it is the greatest investment since the dawn of time, and the world is about to fall into complete helter-skelter. Prepare!

Here are my instructions to you. Call Goldline.com. Ask one of their salesmen the simple question: "If I buy gold, when do I ever sell gold?"

I have done it. Their answer is pure comedy. A 20-something bright-eyed salespeople responded to me: "Gold has never crashed." He added: "If gold was to go again from $800 to $200 you would have plenty of warning to sell." "Who was going to give me that warning?" I asked. He said, drum roll please: "They would."

Everyone should call and have that conversation. Block your number and only give your first name. Ask them the same questions and don't give any personal details. Ordinary people, the backbone of every economy, require encouragement and reassurance, not doomsday theories. Goldline.com is selling Judgement Day fear. It's bogus.

Oh, I forgot. Goldline.com is not selling you the actual gold, or gold futures contracts, or gold ETFs. They are selling you gold coins—often marked up by a huge margin of the actual melt value of the coins. However, I don't want the government telling Goldline that it is illegal to sell gold coins at a crazy premium to inept investors. We have enough busy-body regulations. However, I have no problem making sure my readers see through this dog-and-pony show.

Do trend followers trade gold? Absolutely. When it is going up, they are *long*. When it is going down, they are *short*. They follow the trend. They don't trade because the Mayan calendar is predicting the end of the world in 2012. And if the world does end in 2012, you can't take your coins with you.

> Some attack trend following: "Trend Following is one of the stock market's biggest cons; I would even go so far to compare the concept to a cult, like Scientology. I get the same sort of value from Trend Following as I do from supernatural operators such as Uri Geller and horoscope readers."[2]

*Maria Bartiromo circa 2001:
"I am of the belief that the individual out there is actually not throwing money at things that they do not understand, and is actually using the news and using the information out there to make smart investment decisions."[1]*

Intoxication

A bipolar prediction came across my desk recently: "If the market rises over the next several weeks, today will have been a good day to buy. However, no one can know the answer today. Every day there seems to be a surprise. We don't know how to predict the behavior of foreign countries or their attacks."

The nonsense doesn't stop there. While on the East Coast recently, I was listening to an AM radio finance show. An older man called in to ask how he could buy into various commodity markets. He was worried that they had run too far already. The female host assured him that there was plenty of time and to jump into the market. The caller mentioned that he liked to buy low and was waiting for a pullback. The host told him to start preparing for hyperinflation. She named an African country to enhance her theory and leaned the conversation toward food insurance, needed of course for the coming descent into anarchy.

Think not knowing what you are talking about is new? Think again. President Herbert Hoover circa May 1930: "While the crash only took place six months ago, I am convinced we have now passed through the worst—and with continued unity of effort we shall rapidly recover. There has been no significant bank or industrial failure. That danger, too, is safely behind us."

Can't just pick on old-timers. Consider the current day. Lloyd Blankfein (head of Goldman Sachs) said his firm would have survived the credit crisis without government help. The firm's president, Gary Cohn, was more definitive: "I think we would not have failed. We had cash." Treasury Secretary Timothy Geithner countered, "None of them would have survived" without government help.[2]

More contradicting rhetoric from a 2010 *60 Minutes* interview reinforces the propaganda spell cast:

> **Scott Pelley**: "Is keeping inflation in check less of a priority for the Federal Reserve now?"
>
> **Ben Bernanke**: "No, absolutely not. What we're trying to do is achieve a balance. We've been very, very clear that we will not allow inflation to rise above two percent or less."
>
> **Pelley**: "Can you act quickly enough to prevent inflation from getting out of control?"

Bernanke: "We could raise interest rates in 15 minutes if we have to. So, there really is no problem with raising rates, tightening monetary policy, slowing the economy, reducing inflation, at the appropriate time. Now, that time is not now."

Pelley: "You have what degree of confidence in your ability to control this?"

Bernanke: "One hundred percent."[3]

That confidence seems misplaced when you consider Bernanke's words but a few years before:

In 2005, Bernanke said: "We've never had a decline in house prices on a nationwide basis. So, what I think is more likely is that house prices will slow, maybe stabilize, might slow consumption spending a bit. I don't think it's going to drive the economy too far from its full employment path, though."[4]

In 2006, Bernanke said: "Housing markets are cooling a bit. Our expectation is that the decline in activity or the slowing in activity will be moderate, that house prices will probably continue to rise."[5]

In 2007, Bernanke stated: "At this juncture...the impact on the broader economy and financial markets of the problems in the subprime markets seems likely to be contained."[6]

Worse yet? Bernanke told the Senate Banking Committee in March 2011 that he saw "little evidence" that the stock market was a bubble, but provided *certainty* with this ditty of a response: "Of course, nobody can know for sure." Why again do we care what this man says?

> We inhabit a complex system that has virtually nothing to do with the neoclassical model taught in Econ 101. That's why economists failed to predict the financial crisis.[7]

But before Bernanke, Alan Greenspan was also laying the groundwork. From recently released 2005 documents comes former Atlanta Federal Reserve President Jack Guynn:

"Nearly every major city in Florida has experienced increases in the double-digit range, and some, like Miami, Palm Beach, Sarasota, and West Palm, have been reporting increases in housing prices on a year-over-year basis of between 25 and 30 percent. I'm reasonably comfortable characterizing the housing feeding frenzy in some of our markets as being a bubble or a near bubble. The ugly picture we have seen before—and that they think we may very likely see again before long—goes something like this: The drying up of sales of new units; the painful decision of developers to go ahead and complete the construction of additional units to make them saleable, further depressing the market; and speculators who had hoped to see big capital gains walking away or defaulting on their contracts, giving their properties back to the lender. Perhaps it's because of where I sit, but I am less comforted than some of my colleagues about the housing situation."

Former Chairman Greenspan responded:

"Let's take a break for coffee."[8]

Six years later, in 2011, Alan Greenspan declared:

"I conclude that the current government activism is hampering what should be a broad-based robust economic recovery, driven in significant part by the positive wealth effect of a buoyant U.S. and global stock market."[9]

He means by government activism...QE2? But if there were none of that, would there be a *buoyant* stock market? Isn't Greenspan the chief architect for the *wealth effects* over the last decade in stocks and real estate?

The media are right there too. During production, my documentary film arranged for an interview with CNBC's Maria Bartiromo.

> It took Greenspan.
> It took zero interest rates.
> It took an amazing repackaging of mortgage instruments. It took people begging other people to take equity out of their house to buy another one in Florida.[10]

The interview was approved for months. Other interviews for the film included two Nobel Prize winners, and several legendary hedge fund managers. Bartiromo canceled minutes before her interview. She left a voicemail message:

"I probably should not have said yes to it without having this stuff go through my, uhhh, PR people. I'm sorry about that, but, ah, given what's gone on and all the criticism of analysts and the, you know, the Dot-com boom and bust I...I can't, um, I...I don't want to really do this open ended without really knowing more details."

Bartiromo is a media professional who has interviewed world leaders and top financial experts for more than a decade. However, almost eight years after the Dot-com bubble, Bartiromo was using *it* as a reason to not go on the record about the role media plays on Wall Street. That voicemail confirmed my experiences at CNBC earlier in the year. When they walk off the set, it is just that—a set.

One reader was not happy with my revelations: "You make accusations without any proof or examples. You are media and just as guilty as those you accuse. This is a hatchet piece without merit. You apparently have an audience that hates America, CNBC, and Maria. Glad I don't have to live in your [—-]hole."

It all comes down to propaganda and the battle against it. Anyone familiar with the inner workings of a Tupperware party knows all about the power of influence, and how very well it works.[11]

> **This time it truly is different. Expect the VIX of the policy instrument now known as the stock market to hit 0 as volatility in FX, rates, and commodities approaches asymptote.**[13]

Most info-Web-media-newspaper types don't believe that great trend trading knowledge and wisdom are found by removing junk from people's heads.[12] Removing junk is just as much a part of my calling as explaining the concepts and rules of systematic trend following trading.

You have to understand;
most of these people
are not ready
to be unplugged.
And many of them are
so inured, so hopelessly
dependent on the
system, that they will
fight to protect it.[1]

Parliament of Whores

Social Security is dead? Easier said than done.

On *Meet the Press* in 2010, one United States governor appeared confused: "If you care about democracy and what the everyday citizen believes, and you want to empower them, they don't want the Social Security system to be dismantled, and they don't want the Medicare system to be dismantled...this is a compact between generations to be able to make sure that all of our seniors have the funds when they retire, that they're not going to be homeless, so they're not going to have to go to a shelter."

Did she know that the inflation adjusted return of Social Security is just 2 percent? A United States Senator on *Meet the Press* in 2011 apparently did not: "Social Security is a program that works. It is fully funded for the next 40 years. Stop picking on Social Security. It's not a crisis. Social Security is fine."

Those politicians are not stupid; rather, they have ceased to think. Or, do they just need to tell a certain story to ensure power for whatever party with which they are affiliated? Waiting or hoping for your politician, on the right or the left or anywhere in between, to win an election is an investment strategy of your ignorance.

Behind the scenes and in the halls of Congress; drunks, perverts, and losers addicted to fame and power.

Both sides.

Some history is in order for all those who like to reward and/or blame politicians. Go back to the first war in Iraq. President Bush Sr. had an 89 percent approval rating on February 28, 1991. Then the economy tanked. His fault? No. Real estate crashed in the early 1990s, not long after the savings-and-loan debacle of the late 1980s. What happened next? President William J. Clinton won the fall 1992 election. However, Clinton's election did not signal roaring economic times, and Democrats lost the House and Senate to Republicans for the first time in 40 years in 1994. Did Clinton sink the economy in that short time? No.

Then magic happened. During late 1994, the Internet started to roll, and in August 1995 Netscape went public, a trigger still felt today. Stock markets boomed during 1995–1999. The Dot-com bubble was on. However, this bubble was a problem and people knew it. Federal Reserve Chairman Alan Greenspan uttered the phrase "irrational exuberance" in a December 1996 speech, but simply pointing out a bubble was only so useful. In fact, he was resoundingly ignored, and even jeered by some in the financial media.

The good times kept rolling. President Clinton had an approval rating of 73 percent on December 19, 1998, six years into his presidency. Did he or the Republican Congress have anything to do with record tax receipts coming into government coffers? No. The Dot-com bubble was spinning off cash to everyone. Governments were flush. America was feeling rich.

Party over. The Nasdaq crashed in March 2000. The Fed, knowing the massive problem on their hands and deathly afraid that the Dow would deflate, started cutting the Fed Funds rate of over 6 percent on May 16, 2000, to a low of 1 percent in June 2003. If the Dot-com bubble had not popped in the spring of 2000, would Al Gore have been president? Perhaps, but the fall of 2000 instead brought another President Bush, George W.

President George W. Bush inherited the Dot-com bubble implosion, and less than a year into office, 9/11 hit. Two wars of choice followed. However, Fed rate cutting had already started a new bubble blowing. This time real estate and the Dow were zooming up. People rewarded Bush for the economy even though it was the middle of another bubble. His second term started in January 2005.

All is running smoothly until summer 2007, when the new bubble starts to deflate. It finally crashes in October 2008, and President Barack Obama wins the presidency standing at the right place at the right political time. If the economy had not sunk over 2007–2008, would Republican candidate John McCain be president? Probably. The economy could crater again, or not. If it crashes or not, is it all Obama's fault? No. Are you sitting there still thinking the president will fix your portfolio?

Further, look at the Fed Funds rate manipulation over the last 20 years:

Fed Funds rate 5.50 percent on November 15, 1994.

Stock market takes off.

Fed Funds rate 4.75 percent on November 17, 1998.

Fed Funds rate 6.50 percent on May 16, 2000.

Stock market bubble popped March 2000.

The Fed then lowers 13 times.

Fed Funds rate 3.00 percent on September 17, 2001.

Fed Funds rate 1.25 percent on November 6, 2002.

Stock market takes off.

Real estate takes back off.

Fed Funds rate 1.00 percent on June 25, 2003.

The Fed then raises 17 times.

Fed Funds rate 5.25 percent on August 17, 2007.

The Fed then lowers 10 times.

Stock market bubble popped October 2008.

Fed Funds rate 0 percent on December 16, 2008.

Stock market takes off.

Those examples are all government intervention and manipulation, plain and simple. In 2010, Brian Sack, a senior official at the New York Fed, admitted the need to keep stock markets artificially high: "Nevertheless, balance sheet policy can still lower longer-term borrowing costs for many households and businesses, and it adds to household wealth by keeping asset prices higher than they otherwise would be."

> If you close your eyes, the monster will not go away.

The Fed has essentially admitted to operating a Ponzi scheme.[2]

Am I saying to not trade?

No.

A government-manipulated market is still a market.

With all of the extracurricular policy-making of the government aimed at rigging the markets to some unknown *right* level, trend following is the only sanity available. There is no telling what the government will do to push the stock market to whatever level they feel is important. Conversely,

> You lose money and you jump out the window, too bad. It's your problem. Government should realize at the end of the day it's investors who bear responsibility for their investments.[3]

just as the government can push the stock market up, they can push it down. When will that happen? Unknown, but do not bet against it.

Before enlightenment;
chop wood, carry water.
After enlightenment;
chop wood, carry water.[1]

Crowded House

In case you're concerned that this book will create a whole new generation of trend followers who will negatively affect the frequency, direction, and intensity of trends (as well as your ability to make money trading trends), forget it. Here are reasons why systematic trend following will continue to excel:

- Trend followers follow. They don't generate trends. At the beginning or end of a major trend, there may be volatility, but it will be an extremely superficial, temporary effect.[2]
- People play zero-sum games for many reasons. Not all play to win. Hedgers, for example, trade the market for certain reasons. It's portfolio protection for them. Their insurance premium goes to trend following speculators. The hedgers are getting a benefit even when they lose.
- People would no longer buy and hold. Those believing in fundamental analysis (the vast majority of market participants) would have to switch how they trade. They would need to cease buy and hold and/or long-only approaches and start trading as trend followers.
- Most do not "sell short." They trade "long only." That changes when?
- People would have to dump mutual funds. That will be hard with retirement programs literally mandating 100 percent investments in mutual funds.

> The Internet is arbitraging away *everything*. Man's greatest invention is eliminating the need for *people*.
> How will you adjust?

- Most traders don't think about how much to buy or how much to sell. They only worry about when to buy and rarely think about when to sell. That thought process is very hard to break for a mass trend following conversion.
- CNBC, WSJ, Bloomberg, etc. would need to end.
- People would have to disengage their emotions and egos from their trading. However, as long as there are human beings involved in the trading process, there will be excessive reactions and trends to exploit.
- People would need to stop gambling... They might stop eating too.

Frequently the question is asked, "If trend following works so well, why aren't more people doing it?" Acknowledging complete ignorance about the future is tough to accept, admit, and act on, but that is what trend following requires you to do.

I'm a lawyer defending a major record company, and I'm talkin' about Chewbacca. Does that make sense? Ladies and gentlemen, I am not making any sense. None of this makes sense. And so you have to remember, when you're in that jury room deliberatin' and conjugatin' the "Emancipation Proclamation," does it make sense? No. Ladies and gentlemen of this supposed jury, it does not make sense. If Chewbacca lives on Endor, you must acquit!
The defense rests.[1]

Black Box

In science and engineering, a black box is a device, system, or object that can be viewed solely in terms of its input, output, and transfer characteristics without any knowledge of its internal workings; that is, its implementation is "opaque"—hence the "black" part.[2]

David Swensen, one of the so-called respected Wall Street guys (he runs the $17 billion dollar Yale endowment fund), was blunt as he took a swing at trend traders: "We don't invest in quantitative black box models because we simply don't know what they are doing." How could Swensen not understand a simple trend following system?

> This is a game of misses. The guy who misses the best is going to win.[3]

One trend trader countered: "If you are going to give a systems trader the label 'black box' then all those guys predicting the future, at least have the consistency to call them the crystal ball."[4]

Wall Street needs a spin or a narrative to sell, and they all sell similar stories. Pension funds, family offices, fund of funds, and others who allocate money, like to herd. These gatekeepers always move in lockstep. They blindly follow the worst investing schemes, and continually knock sound strategies such as trend following—with terms like black box.[5]

Why? So many are motivated by what matters least. Namely, quick money (the quicker the better) at whoever's expense. That's how the financial world got so close to the abyss. Many well-intentioned people, running retirement programs with your money, don't know they don't know—and they are prone to investing in the wrong things—regularly.

> Many on Wall Street don't want above average returns. Their objective is to charter the 150 footer, and party like it's 1999. Have you been to Monaco during the Grand Prix? It's a Wall Street orgy.[6]

You say this talk is not related to you? You just have a public pension fund? Not so fast. From state of Texas employees to state of California employees to employees at Verizon and GM to investments made on behalf of police, firemen, and teachers—millions have investments that touch hedge funds. The question: Is your hedge fund investment properly using systematic trend following or is it promising Madoff-like returns?

If man is five/
If man is five/
If man is five/
Then the devil is six/
Then the devil is six
Then the devil is six/
Then the devil is six/
Then the devil is six/
Then god is seven/
Then god is seven/
Then god is seven/
This monkey's
gone to heaven.[1]

Lucky Monkey

"It is easy to locate a bunch of trend followers in hindsight, and tout their abilities. What would be harder would be to find the whole universe of people following trends, and see how they do as a whole."

The last man standing: Lucky survivor or skill?

Evaluate George Soros. His trading has always resembled trend trading. So was Soros just lucky at his trading? Consider this: The probability of George Soros's returns coming from randomness is much smaller than Warren Buffett's, for example, because Soros did almost everything. Buffett on the other hand followed a strategy to buy a few companies that had a certain earnings profile, and it worked for him. There was much more luck involved in Buffett's strategy as he made far fewer decisions.[2]

One reader wrote me: "Suppose we have an infinite number of monkeys each in front of an infinite number of typewriters. We should not be surprised if one of these monkeys eventually produces an identical copy of some great work of fiction. Given the large number of investment products and traders in the world it is perhaps not surprising that there exists a lucky few who turn out to have amazing results. I am not saying the individuals who have produced impressive track records are not skilled but what I am saying is that they may not be as skilled as you think."

Here is a thought for skeptics: Assume that only one lonely trend following trader exists. Just one guy exists who has literally made tens of thousands of trades (if not more) over the course of 40 years as a systematic trend following trader. Assume this hypothetical trend following trader has produced nearly +20 percent per year on average. Yes, that is a serious number—especially when compounded.

> When I was in elementary school, we had the kid who threw chairs, the kid who stuttered, and the kid who went to the bathroom on himself, but we never had the kid who came in one day and started shooting everyone.[3]

As you may have guessed—he is real.

To suggest that there is nothing to be learned from trend following performance success across many, many traders, spanning decades, in all types of markets, both up and down trends, is absurd. The life-changing question for you: Is there anything to learn from the numerous winning trend following traders, or do you view them as just lucky monkeys whose darts happened to hit all bull's-eyes for decades?

This is the fork in the road for you: luck or skill. The choice will alter your life.

A good traveler has no fixed plans and is not intent on arriving.[1]

Honest

Mutual funds, brokers, financial news, big banks, and 23-year-old AP finance writers fresh out of journalism school, the ones who literally make up the fundamental news and predictions daily, have all been a massive sham, wittingly or unwittingly, and to say that puts a .30-06 bullseye figuratively between my eyes.

Provoke reactions. Cause some to whine. Yes, that's what I do. Here are some *friends*:

- The [trend following] field is marked by unsubstantiated claims of success; a track record of failure and associated rationalizations; a lack of peer reviewed studies showing any positive results; and a collection of logical, mathematical and statistical fallacies. Although there are plenty of technical traders having success, there is no evidence that they are anything more than statistical artifact and the hidden use of standard, subjective, fundamental analysis. Technical traders fail to realize that the market would quickly overwhelm any truly successful system, rendering it useless.[2]

> The Ramones sang, "There's no stoppin' the cretins from hoppin'."

- [Covel's] book does not say how to be a trend follower, or how the average person can buy commodities, FX, futures etc., the markets trend followers use. I hate books that promote stuff, but then don't actually tell you anything or how to do it.
- Trend following is one of the stock market's biggest con; I would even go so far to compare the concept to a cult like Scientology.
- There were no specifics. No rocks to cling on to. If you want to discover trend following techniques then look elsewhere.
- [*Trend Following*] has no substance. Lots of historic data to show trend following does exist, some people make money doing it, but no more! It has zero information on how to do it.
- You'll find in [Covel's] books a kind of anti-intellectualism shared by many blind-faith religious people.
- BEWARE: Covel had an agenda when he wrote [*The Complete TurtleTrader*].

- Rather than impartially presenting the evidence, like any good evangelical sectarian blind-faither, [Covel] pitches the story as one of competition between two mutually incompatible doctrines.

- Examining only price action is clearly a kind of primitive attempt. The analogy I think of is in trying to explain the movement of oceanic water. Examining nothing other than the surface phenomena of price action is analogous to looking at surface wave movements only—where the wind explains some part of the movement. Now what might really be moving bodies of water requires a fundamental model—for example, how gravity, the moon, ocean floor structure, temperature might explain the movement of oceanic water mass.

- [Covel's] documentary [*Broke: The New American Dream*] does not address the saps who haven't been drawn the cards on the table to put them in the game of risk and luck depicted here. It presumes that millions of other dwellers beyond the devastated areas have sufficient income to generate their American Dream. It begs you to have the mental aptitude of a Houdini. It wants us to believe that life has affordable risks if we have the instincts of a poker player; whereas, until the 70s, the American Dream was guaranteed by an education, solid marriage, and sound character. Here, you only require the predatory instincts of a roving gambler. Welcome to West World, by gummy!

- [Covel], there is no contradiction between being a chartist, an Elliottician, and a trend follower. I consider myself all of the above, as well as a fundamentalist.

> **If you understand, things are just as they are.**
> **If you do not understand, things are just as they are.**

One of the most useful criticisms that you can use to further your understanding centers on *prediction*. Trend followers, as shown throughout *Trend Commandments*, do not predict a market's timing or direction. Trend followers react to market movements. It is critical distinction best seen in the words of trend follower Bill Dunn:

> "We don't make market predictions. We just ride the bucking bronco."

One critic could not wrap his arms around the idea. He yelled and he beat his chest in argument for quite a long time. However, you need to judge whether Bill Dunn, a man with a 35-year performance track record, and who has made hundreds of millions in profit as a trend following trader, is wrong with his *no prediction* wisdom or whether my critic, who works as a massage therapist, is right with his trend followers *do predict* wisdom.

However, even after the last decade of market tumult, the media still push the prediction party line:

"The markets may be rational after all. The threat of severe nuclear contamination from a breached Japanese nuclear reactor still looms. The outcome of the escalating war in Libya is uncertain. Yet The Standard & Poor's 500 index ended the week up 2.7 percent. The Dow Jones industrial average rose 3.1 percent. So what happened to all that headline-driven volatility from two weeks ago? If you look at historical patterns, this week's rebound isn't so surprising. The numbers suggest stocks will likely keep rising for the next few months."[3]

It is guaranteed that if you think you can forecast the future, you will lose your shirt betting on those predictions.

Some will never *know* and will rip this book as well. A famed Stanford University psychologist has said that a man with a conviction is a hard man to change. Tell him you disagree and he turns away. Show him facts or figures and he questions your sources. Appeal to logic and he fails to see your point.

> My role is not Dr. Phil's. Some critics' issues might be best left for their therapist.

Now I could very easily avoid criticism, do nothing, say nothing, and be nothing, but quitting is not in my DNA.

However, criticism is important and often invigorating for many reasons:

- You are on the right track when a target appears on your back.

- Making a sizable dent in public thought brings detractors and saboteurs. It's part of doing business.[4]

- Trying to get everyone to like you is mediocrity.[5]

- You are going to be criticized if you play small or play big. Might as well play big. Criticism will come either way.[6]

- History does not remember those who pretend to be neutral. Picking sides, choosing those you want to be associated with, and sticking with your true beliefs is all that counts.[7]

- Speaking out on issues, that others are too afraid to do, will draw criticism.[8]
- Disgruntled people need to release anger. Standing there as an easy outlet for their anger is part of the gig. Criticism always parallels influence.[9]
- It takes courage to see things for what they are, not what you want them to be.
- Poking an inferiority complex brings out vitriol—always.

Hit me.[10]

Society's insatiable push to discredit those who rock the boat, coupled with digital printing presses cataloging it all, has allowed village idiots and Nobel Prize winners to effectively share the same stage. In this environment, for many, the truth has ceased to matter.

If you were to put all trend following models side by side, you would probably find that most made profits and incurred losses in the same markets. They were all looking at the same charts and obtaining the same perception of opportunity.[1]

Under the Radar

My second book, *The Complete TurtleTrader*, was the true story of a group of novices who were hired in the early 1980s and trained to be trend following traders by one of the legendary traders of all time—Richard Dennis. They were nicknamed the *Turtles*. Many of them still trade today and are acknowledged to be some of the best trend traders around. This is actually grounded in a real-life experiment like in the film *Trading Places*—taking people off the street and turning them into millionaires.

There was one TurtleTrader who was impossible to find during my book research process. I later discovered he was an accomplished guitarist specializing in acoustic, Klezmer, and Latin music. Does he still trade? Yes, said one of his fellow Turtle traders. That same Turtle told me that this guitar-teaching-trend-following Turtle has had the best returns for any Turtle since 1988.

> There are people making money in the markets through skill. They're just not writing papers about it.[2]

You go to college. You decide to take music classes studying guitar. Unbeknownst to you, your teacher is secretly one of the best trend following traders alive today. Crazy world. How many students at San Diego State would ever know the man playing guitar in the university quad knows more about trading and making money than the entire business faculty at the university?

The dog days are over/
The dog days are done/
The horses are coming/
So you better run.[1]

Ethos

The very bright trailblazers who molded my thinking can be seen across these pearls:

- Bring joyful, imaginative, and impassioned energy every day. Don't fake it.
- You don't need to be big to be good, you need to be smart.
- When there is no one there, insert yourself. Take over.
- Engage the world as if your life depends on it.
- Nothing is more important than transforming someone.
- Have a vision grounded in your uniqueness.
- The race winner is often curious and slightly mad.
- Dry obligation in life will figuratively kill you.
- No one will give you permission. Seize the mantle.
- If you can't solve a problem, you are playing by the collective's rules.
- Hard work, sustained concentration, and drive are the so-called *secrets*.
- Winners understand sunk costs and opportunity costs.
- Plan to win, prepare to win, and have every right to expect to win.
- It's in your power to change your belief systems. No one is stuck. Be unstuck.

These are not easy. Society is not organized to encourage and celebrate the unproven striver. It is much safer to beat up the new thought or heap scorn upon it. Too many young minds are encouraged to take a *safe* path. Years ago, this was solid advice. Today, this is awful advice. It is shortsighted.[2]

> If you are any good, the *man* will spot you and *not* want you.

And for those who complain they were born without a silver spoon, who think they need more money to start, who say that they were not blessed to have trend following rules in their early twenties (like the famous TurtleTraders), money cannot compensate for a lack of talent, for sloth, a flawed vision, or for a pedestrian frame of mind.[3]

Here is a great example of not being lodged in a pedestrian way. Michael Rosenberg of *Sports Illustrated* was reflecting on Cinderellas Butler and Virginia Commonwealth University (VCU) both advancing to the 2011

NCAA Final Four. If you recall, both these teams had rocky seasons and were not locks to make the tournament till the very end of their seasons. He noted that it was a good thing to sprint to the edge of a cliff and stop:

> "If you almost get eliminated, two wonderful things can happen. One, you know you can handle the pressure, and you don't worry about it anymore. And two, you feel like it's your destiny to win. I don't believe in destiny, but I believe in believing in destiny. What I mean is that a team that believes in its destiny is more likely to win. We're all surprised that those guys...are in the Final Four. But they don't seem surprised, and maybe that helps explain why they are [there]."[4]

I tend to think of myself as a one-man wolf pack.[6]

Nothing can keep you from winning, if winning is what you really want to do. To think otherwise suggests not just a lack of imagination but also a failure of the optimism necessary for attracting good things. No optimism? Throw this book away immediately.[5]

Everybody's talking and
no one says a word/

Everybody's making love
and no one really cares/

Everybody's running and
no one makes a move/

Everyone's a winner and
nothing left to lose/

Strange days indeed,
most peculiar mama.[1]

Games People Play

You can make your first million—and that is the hard number. Anyone can do it. Of course, billions, and degrees of billions, require some luck. However, an educated person, no matter how they get their education, can indeed saddle up to their iPad and make a small fortune. To say otherwise is disingenuous.

The world has changed. The game is different. If you are sitting around waiting for a job to magically appear, or if you are listening to talking heads rambling on about politicians creating jobs, or worse yet, you think China is the enemy to your wealth creation, it has to be asked: *"Are you a masochist?"*

It is time to incite the conversation. Disrupt the status quo. Push people off the matrix. Spark curiosity. And do it differently.

There is another game to play. Trend following trading is that game, but it is terribly important to avoid becoming the game—a game I have explained in a multitude of ways. So think about the three types of players in any game:

- Those who know they are in the game.
- Those who do not know they are in the game.
- Those who do not know they are in the game and have become the game.[2]

When you walk into the room, if you don't know who the mark is—you are the mark.[3]

Within a half hour of playing any game, if you do not know the patsy, you are it. Said another way: *You are the game.* That is serious talk for the serious game of your financial health and wealth.

**Rommel,
you magnificent
bastard,
I read your book!**[1]

Blood Hound

People spend so much time listening to someone else feed information. Then they are judged at how well they regurgitate it back to whomever offered it. It is almost like a college drinking game—that is, the level of sophistication involved.

When it comes time to take responsibility for decision-making, many seem to be waiting for an order. Or, peeking over their shoulder to see what others are doing just to ensure they are doing something similar. Curiosity has been

Not clever or gifted, just curious.

lobotomized from too many. Freud lamented: "What a distressing contrast between the radiant intelligence of a child and the feeble mentality of the average adult."

Simple childlike curiosity with no agenda except to know—that's *it*—is a precious commodity. Kids have that wide-eyed wonderment when they take apart their first toy to figure out how it works—and so should you. As simplistic as it sounds, maintaining childlike wonder and enthusiasm keeps your mental doors open.

A top CEO recently spoke before a Harvard MBA class. One of the students asked, "What do I do?" The CEO replied, "Take the rest of the money you have not spent on tuition and do something else." If you do not understand his wisdom, fine. If you are curious, though, you will figure it out. That is the difference.

However, with so many conditioned as lemmings, they have become scared to death to be curious. They worry that by asking questions they will be exposed as less than. In truth, by not questioning the world, you always lose. Still others might not fear the question, but instead fear the answer. It's a vicious circle.

Open-ended curiosity lets you take a step back and see everything for what it is right now. Curiosity is the only reason this book exists. It forced me to dig deeper. Taking very little at face value has always been my modus operandi. Do you really think teachers liked it when I raised my hand?

> The phrases *gifted musician,*
> *natural athlete,* and *innate*
> *intelligence* are genetic prisons.
> Abilities are not set in genetic
> stone. They are soft and
> sculptable, far into adulthood.
> With humility, hope, and
> extraordinary determination,
> greatness is something everyone
> can aspire to.[2]

Challenging accepted norms has always been my passion. Unearthing details that some may have wanted buried has made me pretty damn good at navigating obscure fields unrelated to trading—like State and Federal open records law.

In this small world, one of the more unlikely people to have asked me, "How do you go about unearthing details?" was Mikhail Gorbachev. The former president had been told in Russian that my career involved profiling traders who make the big money, so when an introduction was made, he asked me in Russian through a translator, "What is it like to write about these traders?" Realizing his time was limited, my response was short: "Very interesting," I said. He waited for the translation and asked back: "It must be difficult to get behind the scenes; how do you do it?" With a smile, "Oh, I am very good at digging." He laughed. No translation was needed. He understood my English perfectly.[3]

Many ask me Gorbachev's question.

Followed by: "How do I know I can be a trend follower?"

And followed by: "How do I know you can help me learn?"

My education comes directly from some of the great trend traders of the last five decades. No hyperbole there, just a fact. However, it did not start that way. It started while finishing graduate school in London circa 1994. A book by motivational speaker Anthony Robbins convinced me that getting close to great traders was a path to pursue. Sounded easy, but how was I going to do it? One part of Robbins's book really struck me.

Unlimited Power featured a story about director Steven Spielberg. His life changed when he took a tour of Universal Studios at the age of 17. The tour didn't make it to where all the action was, so Spielberg took his own action. He sneaked off to watch the filming of a real movie. Later, he ended up meeting the head of Universal's editorial department, who expressed an interest in one of his early films. For most people, that is where the story would have ended, but Spielberg wasn't like most. He kept pushing by meeting directors, writers, and editors, learning from every conversation, observing, and developing more and more sensory acuity about what worked in moviemaking.[4]

That Spielberg story was all the motivation needed. Example: I once flew to Berlin, Germany, spending thousands of dollars not in my bank account, just for the chance to possibly meet and learn from a few traders at a conference—a conference where no one knew me. My credentials were a nametag and moxy, but that calculated gamble worked out enough to find myself spending quality time with a former chairman of the Chicago Mercantile Exchange.

Those conferences allowed face-to-face access to legendary traders— enough personal contact that even Dustin Hoffman's character in *Rain Man* could see that they put their pants on like everyone else. Attendance at those conferences triggered my confidence and passion.

Unfortunately, we have a culture where that *go figure it out* attitude is not the norm. In today's world, children grow up with soccer leagues and spelling bees where everyone gets a *prize*. On the playgrounds, dodge ball has been deemed too *traumatic*. Some lactose intolerant parents consider musical chairs dangerously *exclusionary*. Kids are constantly praised for routine accomplishments.[5]

> No one is going to know or care about your failures. All you have to do is learn from them because all that matters is that you get it right once. Then everyone can tell you how lucky you were.[6]

Those kids will never be curious. They will probably end up addicted to Xanax-Ritalin sprinkled cupcakes so they can *cope*. Am I being a pessimistic grouch? Far from it—just describing the playing field and your opponents.

If I leave here tomorrow/
Would you still remember me/
For I must be traveling on now/
There's too many places
I've got to see.[1]

Epilogue

While watching David Duchovny's *Californication* and hearing Lynyrd Skynyrd's "Free Bird" in the background credits (can't make that combination up), my fascination started anew. Adrenaline pumped. That random stimulation was a reminder that nothing is traditional about my so-called "Wall Street" research career. Accidental tourist. Yes, that sounds about right. No formal training. No rulebook. An ordainment by powers that be never came, nor was it expected.

Trend Commandments started as a reimagining of my first book. I wanted to break *Trend Following* open and make it more digestible, less academic. Using my best pseudo Jay-Z sampling skills, I have tried to create a unique work with *Trend Commandments* built around timeless principles and a unique access.

> This book is not just my view. It is 15 years of osmosis with great trend following traders. It is a behind-the-curtain treatise.

Today, top traders share with me. Practice, hard work, and just pulling my chair up to the table fixed once-insurmountable access barriers. It has been a circuitous journey, one step forward, two steps back, four steps forward. One random data point connected to other random data points, in ways with seemingly no connection.

Not surprisingly, it was a chance meeting with a legend in the trend following world that shifted my gluteus maximus into overdrive. Dateline 2001. Interestingly, this get-together only happened because my firm had registered his name as a domain name. Not to cybersquat, but the business telescope looking ahead thought it might lead to a biography web site, but there was no real plan. When he first e-mailed asking for the domain, the ownership paperwork was signed over and sent along to him for nothing.

A short while later, he reached out. A friendship unfolded. Business ideas were discussed. At one point, an associate of his approached about acquiring my firm. The three of us were in on an e-mail conversation discussing specifics. This new trader friend of mine responded to his associate:

"If Mike is the real thing, and he seems to act like it, then you can't get him as an employee and you can't get his work as an acquisition. You just wind up getting the car without an engine, the engine without a piston, the spark plug without the spark. I'm more in favor of the symbiosis approach than in the assimilation approach, trying to take over, dominate and run everyone our firm comes in contact with. You just wind up being able to take over dependent types. Good fences make good neighbors. Good neighbors help each other. I think he is a good ol' boy with a lot of energy and lots of sense, and I think he fits in very nicely as part of our valuable good ol' boy network. Of course, you could likely convince me otherwise by showing me your pro-forma cash-flow spreadsheet of how it is possible to live long and prosper by controlling Mike & www.turtletrader.com in such a way that our firm can *own* entrepreneurs."

His message, wit, and sarcasm said clearly it was smarter for me to go it alone. That e-mail dramatically influenced and reinforced my entrepreneurial core. Far more than comatose time spent in my MBA program, his e-mail set in motion the confidence for my first book *Trend Following* and the projects that followed.

> 1-2-3 Kill![2]

Ten years later, following others or being controlled by others is still not a game worth accepting. Nobody should accept control as you only live one time. There are no do-overs.

However, that experience had a recent bookend. After bumping into each other several times, and after having several requisite "how's the weather" conversations, and knowing a little bit about each other through mutual acquaintances, a particular woman approached me and said simply, "You are an author?"

> You have a real life if and only if you do not compete with anyone in any of your pursuits.[3]

Well, for myself that is an odd question and not so easy to answer. My mind raced with ways. Author? "No, more of an entrepreneur." "Author doesn't fit." The brain starts going back and forth, and momentarily it was forgotten that a conversation was still going on with her. She saw the hesitation and fired with sharp wit, **"So you are not sure what you are?"**

Acta est fabula

Extras

Every bet you make with your money
involves a decision to risk something of value, time, money,
or emotional involvement for an uncertain prospect of gain.
Placing winning bets over the long run
requires constant decisions in the face of
innumerable trade-offs.
That is life and the trend following life.

Whether sunny or bleak, convictions about the future satisfy the hunger for certainty. We want to believe. And so we do.[1]

Surprise, Surprise, Surprise

Earlier in the chapter "Systematic Trend Following," I included a small excerpt from CNBC's Erin Burnett interviewing trend following trader David Harding a few years back. On April 8, 2011, CNBC anchor Joe Kernen interviewed Harding as well. At the time of that interview, Harding's firm Winton Capital was managing $21 billion dollars in assets for clients via trend following strategies. Now that you have read *Trend Commandments*, consider Kernen's interview and my questions that follow.

Kernen started the interview reading from a piece of paper that described Harding as a systematic trend follower who believes scientific research will succeed in the long run. He wondered out loud if "computers" were used and asked Harding to describe his trading strategy.[2]

Harding, on remote from London, responded that his firm "goes with the flow." He follows trends and makes money going *long* on rising markets and *short* on declining markets. He mentioned that there had been enough trends for his firm to make money *nearly* every year for the last 15 years.[3]

Kernen pounced, wondering whether he could blame Harding and other trend followers for Oil and Gold going higher and "for the pendulum swinging much further than it should on a fundamental basis."[4] Harding thought there might be some truth to Kernen's point, but there was only so much time to elaborate. Kernen, under his breath, with a huge wide smile emerging, interjected at that acknowledgement: "Uh, yeah."[5]

> The ancients were known to engage in reading entrails of animals to forecast the future.

Harding reminded Kernen that his firm was limited by speculative position limits set by the government and that his trading size was tiny by comparison to major investment banks. Harding went on to further clarify that he doesn't trade by a "gut feel." He added: "We don't just make it up." He also didn't apologize for his scientific approach to markets, an approach he defined as "rigorous."[6]

> Markets are not efficient or orderly. They are an endless battleground. Opposing views fighting each other to a standstill until one side eventually prevails and surges ahead. The emergence of price trends often reflects the end of a battle.[7]

Kernen replied with a shot across the bow bringing up failed hedge fund Long Term Capital Management (LTCM). He saw it as ironic that LTCM folded in the same year (1997) that Harding's firm launched: "I heard *science* and I heard you've never had a down year, and it just reminded me of LTCM." Kernen talked sarcastically about the Nobel Prize winners at LTCM, their "algorithms," and the fact that they never had a down year until their blowup.[8]

Harding quickly clarified that his firm did have a down year in 2009 and that his performance success actually went back over two decades—23 years to be exact. He noted that his first firm AHL (which he sold) was now the world's largest managed futures fund. He also addressed LTCM head-on, stating that the book *When Genius Failed* (the story of LTCM blowing up) was "required reading" at his firm.[9]

Kernen, with condescension, quipped: "I bet it is." He then went on to ask Harding if he could provide some of his best "picks." That question makes perfect sense for every fundamental trader who thinks he can predict the future, but it is a ridiculous question to ask a trend following trader. Harding replied that he could not forecast markets: "I can't give you best picks." He pointed out that his success comes from having a slight *edge* and proper *betting*.[10]

Kernen, still not about to acknowledge anything positive about trend following, smugly asked if Harding would know when the party was over. Harding was nonplussed, noting that there has been a long history of successful trend following going back 40 years. He also compared 2010-2011's great trending markets to another era—the 1970s.[11]

Kernen, with little journalistic objectivity, shot back that he had heard those kinds of expressions before: "'Please let there be another real estate boom because I spent all the money I made.' I heard commodities guys saying that for a while [too]." He then wrapped up with standard pleasantries and one last zinger hoping that Harding could come back again "with the same moniker [and] same title."[12]

Before analyzing the interview, consider a definition of *critical thinking*:

"Critical thinking is the intellectually disciplined process of actively and skillfully conceptualizing, applying, analyzing, synthesizing, and/or evaluating information gathered from, or generated by, observation, experience, reflection, reasoning, or communication, as a guide to belief and action. In its exemplary form, it is based on universal intellectual values that transcend subject matter divisions: clarity, accuracy, precision, consistency, relevance, sound evidence, good reasons, depth, breadth, and fairness."[13]

With that in mind, here are some questions to ponder:

1. Is it believable that Joe Kernen, the anchor of CNBC's longest running program, had no knowledge and/or comprehension of trend following, or other descriptions of it such as managed futures or CTAs? If he was forced to raise his right hand under the threat of perjury, do you think he would still have such a limited understanding of trend following and managed futures?
2. When Kernen asked about trend followers purportedly pushing markets further than they *should be* fundamentally, did that mean he had a way to determine the *correct* price level of all markets at all times?
3. When Kernen brought up Long Term Capital Management in attempt to compare Harding to its demise, did he not understand that Harding did not believe in efficient markets? Had he ever looked at a monthly up and down track record of Harding or any trend follower?
4. Why ask a trend following trader for "picks"?
5. When Kernen asked Harding if he would come back with the same moniker and title, was he implying that he believed Harding would blow up soon and be back on CNBC under some reformulated firm name—like what the proprietors of Long Term Capital Management did after their blowup? Has he ever asked Warren Buffett *that* question?

I can easily see some painting this interview differently:

"Harding set himself up for the LTCM tie-in by framing himself as a computer science shop looking at data and being black box."

"You have to expect Kernen to kick you. That's what he does. Just like you know what you're going to get from Glenn Beck or Stephen Colbert."

"Harding basically says, 'We are the smartest guys on the planet, trends work, and we look at a lot of data.'"

One reader, a reader who runs a fundamental advisory service, wrote me:

> "Whether Kernen's questions were clueless or not is really irrelevant. He did not argue with Harding on any point, and he gave Harding a good opportunity (within the time available) to explain how his firm implements trend following. [Kernen] was an 'adult in the room.' I'm thinking that's the way serious trend followers ought to consider presenting themselves instead of sarcasm and 'we don't predict' as if that is an obvious answer to any question."

The evidence does not bear those criticisms out. There is a deeper game at play beyond my questions. Joe Kernen is not devoid of academic intelligence. He holds a bachelor's degree from the University of Colorado in molecular, cellular, and developmental biology and master's degree from Massachusetts Institute of Technology. He worked at several investment banks including Merrill Lynch.

> **Some kids just have to move.**
> **They want it more.**
> **They have no choice.**
> **They must win.**

I am no Harding fanboy or apologist, but I have spent time with him. That research time, coupled with his public career and track record, make him one of the most learned trend trading voices of the past twenty years. It is clear to me that Kernen had a preformulated agenda. His questioning was a transparent attempt to marginalize Harding and trend following. Why would Kernen do that? Imagine if the interview started like this:

> "We at CNBC believe in efficient markets and the use of fundamental analysis. Our business model requires viewers to watch. Today, we have a guest on who has made billions with trend following trading, which does not require fundamental analysis or CNBC. Would you like to know how to make money without ever watching our channel again? Welcome David Harding!"

A Kernen ego will never debate this subject on neutral grounds, but that is no surprise. Learn from this interview and the analysis. For those with their eyes wide open, this is yet another moneymaking confidence builder.

Note: I have excerpted the interview. The unabridged interview can be found here: http://video.cnbc.com/gallery/?video=3000015574.

You can't change the direction of the wind, but you can adjust your sails.

Origins

Stig Ostgaard is a "TurtleTrader"—a trader covered in my second book, The Complete TurtleTrader. *He graciously allowed his history of trend following to be reprinted in* Trend Commandments:

Although trend following has been a popular trading philosophy for many years, surprisingly little has been written about its origins and history. This is partly due, no doubt, to the scarcity of available information prior to the early 20th century, and because until about 50 years ago, trend following as a philosophy had not been completely articulated. To be sure, by the early 1950s, many trend following methodologies were in common use—and may have been for centuries—but the underlying concept had not been fully defined, or even given a name.

One reason for this paucity of early information is suggested by the "following" part of the term "trend following." The implication is one of passivity, of reaction, rather than of bold, assertive action—and human nature shows a distinct preference for the latter. Also, trend following appears to be too simple an idea to be taken seriously. Indeed, simple ideas can take a long time to be accepted—think of the concept of a negative number, or of zero: Simple to us, but problematic to ancestors.

But, for whatever reasons, people learn easily from the past only that which the participants of the time chose to reveal, and above that, what their chroniclers found interesting enough about which to write. People know the stories of the "plungers," the "manipulators," and their "corners"; of Daniel Drew, Jay Gould, James A. Patten, and Arthur Cutten; but little of the lesser-known traders, or "followers," sitting on the sidelines analyzing the markets, perhaps more successfully than their legendary contemporaries. Nevertheless, history is not completely in the dark. There are things to be revealed by looking back into history.

Let's deconstruct the subject. Is trend following one thing, or is it many? Certainly it has—at least today—many manifestations. There are breakout systems, moving average systems, volatility systems, and many others, all of which can be considered to be trend following in nature. But these are the particulars. What are the universals? What is trend following's basic nature?

As a first attempt at definition, I would suggest that trend following has two natures. It is at one level a phenomenon of the human psyche, an expression of the Keynesian "animal spirits" that percolate from the deepest levels of man's being. This type of trend following is spontaneous, inductive, adaptive, and evolutionary—a burst of conformity to innovations in the immediate environment. At this level, the masses have always been trend followers, not only in financial matters, but also in terms of music, art, clothing, and basic worldviews. But the other level of trend following is something else entirely. This is the meta-level, which sits above the tableau of material and psychological cause and effect, allowing participants to observe the behavior of the markets as a whole—and to design intelligent, premeditated responses to market action. This is the level of trend following from which we as traders should and usually do operate.

Now, although trend following at this meta-level can certainly become complex, still its essential elements can be simply stated. They are three: 1) To initiate positions based on the perceived direction of the trend, 2) To hold positions based on the perceived direction of the trend, and 3) To liquidate positions based on the perceived direction of the trend

There is also possibly a fourth thing, as suggested above: It is to do all of these things systematically, on the basis of logical relationships or mathematical formulations. But I do not think that this is an absolute requirement. It is certainly possible to be a subjective trend follower, or to combine systematic and subjective elements in a trend following system. In fact, I believe that some great traders did indeed include subjective elements in their methodologies. Here, however, I will focus on the systematic aspect.

And here again, the systematic nature of trend following can be simply stated. Generally (though not invariably), trend following systems look for their implementation only at the movement of prices. The basic perception is that if a market's price is going to make an exceptional move in one direction or another, it will first make a moderate move in that direction, leading to the conclusion that if an initiation can be made at that moderate level, the remaining portion of the trend can be followed for a significant period of time thereafter and liquidated at a profit. This scenario is not always expected to be true, of course; but if it is true often enough, and to a significant degree enough, then it may lead to profitable trading in the long run.

As much as people can associate trend following with human nature, no one knows who the first trend followers were. But if there is no known beginning, one is created. You can say something about a part of trend following. Specifically, of the three elements of trend following mentioned above— initiation, holding, and liquidation—it is the middle part, staying with the trend, that has had a reasonably long pedigree. A number of the speculators and plungers of the past, when asked about their trading strategies, said that they held on to their positions as long as possible, i.e., they stayed with the trend.

As one example, consider the economist and trader David Ricardo, who flourished in the London markets from the 1790s until about 1818. A large trader in Consols (bonds) and stocks, he accumulated a large fortune from his speculations, which afforded him the leisure to focus on his primary interest in life, economics. Exactly what his methodologies were is not known, but it is to him that one of the most famous sayings in all of trading history is attributed: "Cut short your losses; let your profits run on."[1]

This is good advice, no doubt—it has survived to the present time and is expressed often. Still, there is no detail here, no advice on how to cut losses or how to let profits run on. And while the first part of the maxim says something about some liquidations, nothing is said about initiations. The ending part, however, is a clear exposition of a central tenet of trend following philosophy: As long as the trade is going your way, don't get out.

For another example, move forward a century and west to another continent. Here is a quotation from the famous grain trader of the Chicago pits, Arthur W. Cutten: "Most of my success has been due to my hanging on while my profits mounted. There is the big secret. Do with it what you will."[2]

Again, Cutten is saying, "stay with the trend."

For a third and final example, let us introduce Jesse Livermore, a very central figure in the history of trend following, about whom more will be said later. Here is a significant quote from him: "...the big money is not in the individual fluctuations but in the main movements—that is, not in reading the tape but in sizing up the entire market and its trend."[3]

This last quote is from Edwin Lefèvre's "Reminiscences of a Stock Operator," a series of articles from the *Saturday Evening Post* in 1922-1923, reprinted in book form many times. Although the speaker is stated to be Larry Livingston, it is generally agreed, based on known biographical information, that Lefèvre's interviewee was Jesse Livermore. The quotation, in turn, is Livermore's interpretation of an oft-repeated statement made by "Old Partridge," a brokerage-house acquaintance of Livermore's, that "It's a bull market, you know." This advice was given whenever some trader was tempted to liquidate a winning position too soon and was not always well regarded. To Livermore, however, the advice finally sank in, yielding the analysis above, and, it would seem, changing his trading style, if not permanently, at least in his periods of trading well. "Old Partridge," alas, though people would like to know a lot more about him, will remain a mystery. How did he initiate his positions? How did he liquidate? No one will probably ever know.

Prior to the mid 19th century, speculation seems to have been largely the province of the elite, and a small coterie of early, but still semi-elite, trend followers. The larger public's participation was primarily as trend followers in the lower sense, taking part in one or another of the "bubbles" that permeated the financial scene from time to time, helping to precipitate the panics that occurred regularly during the period.

But the next half-century and beyond saw the growth of a much larger pool of market participants, as well as some fundamental changes in thinking and procedures. According to William Fowler, in his book *Ten Years in Wall Street* (written in 1870), the key year was 1862, "when began the greatest era of speculation the world has ever seen," while "Uncle Sam's presses were printing greenbacks by the million."[4]

To be sure, some price movements in stocks and commodities during this era were breathtaking: In addition to the grain corners previously mentioned, there was the "gold pool" of 1869, as well as regular bull runs in numerous railroad stocks.

The importance of Fowler to knowledge is that he was not just a writer; he was a participant. He knew the major traders of the day personally and participated in many of the market movements of the day himself. Finally, there is an extensive and meaningful narrative concerning speculation and the workings of the markets during a very formative period.

Significantly, none of these writers records the use of any meaningful systematic trend following methodology, although Fowler does give an example of Pat Hearne, who added to his position every time the price of his stock went up by one percent, and sold out entirely when it went down one percent.[5]

Henry Clews, in *Twenty-eight Years*, suggests a very primitive form of trend following, advising young traders to watch the behavior of the old retired operators who, away from the hustle and bustle and after many, many years of experience finally imbued with wisdom, leave their homes only a few times a year to make their appearances on the Street—at times of market euphoria to sell and in panics to buy. "I say to the young speculators, therefore, watch the ominous visits to the Street of these old men....If you only wait to see them purchase...you can hardly fail to realize handsome profits on your ventures."[6]

Good advice, perhaps. But the problem was actually greater. Rather than "old men," it was the rings and pools that more often began major market moves. How could one tell when a pool had started buying? Or had begun selling? These questions had no real fundamental answer, or at least none that was accessible to the average small trader in these markets. To be sure, there were newspapers, but how was one to know the truth of what was being reported? Even if there was no outright disinformation, surely the big speculators did not telegraph their intents so easily. They rather tried to hide their buying and selling. So, for the small trader, the question was a technical one, to be answered by observing who was doing the buying and selling—to whatever extent that was possible—or by watching the price action of the stock itself, and the volume. And so I would argue that the technical approach to trading, including trend following, came about not by design, but by necessity.

Speculation in the 19th century was, it would appear, rich in practice but poor in theory. What was needed was an approach that could step back from the fray, observe the actions of the marketplace from an objective distance, and contemplate the nature of price fluctuations and swings over the period of days, months, and years. Were there meaningful patterns hiding in the ebb and flow of prices? Could knowledge of these patterns be the basis for trading the markets? Was there a theory that might provide structural, systematic underpinnings for a true trend following model?

In fact, such a model was being developed, if incompletely, as the century was drawing to a close. The model was called Dow Theory, based on concepts originated by Charles H. Dow in a series of articles in the *Wall Street Journal* between 1899 and 1902, expanded upon by William Hamilton between 1903 and 1929, and refined by Robert Rhea in 1932. Inasmuch as Dow Theory defines a bull market as a series of higher highs, and a bear market as a series of lower lows, the rudiments of a trend following strategy become apparent: One buys on the breakout of an old high, and sells on the breakout of an old low. Of course, there are further rules dealing with confirmation and volume, but as a bare bones system, the above will suffice (recognizing, of course, that the methodology can be applied to individual equities and commodities as well as "averages").

The Dow Theory is, I believe, the earliest modern expression of an objective trend following system, inasmuch as it defines precisely—as long as one can define precisely what constitutes a meaningful high or low—the entry and exit levels for trend following trades. Further, the methodology can be generalized and parameterized: Different levels of breakouts can be used, moving averages of prices can be used, etc. Dow Theory is certainly the grandfather of trend following methodologies; indeed, one can argue that subsequent methodologies are mere refinements of it.

Dow Theory itself is not very mathematical; rather, it makes logical observations about current and past prices to determine the direction of the market. This innumeracy is not surprising, since the theory was developed long before the advent of the computer. Nor is it surprising that the earliest offshoots of Dow Theory continued in this observational, structural mode of analysis. Robert Prechter, for example, states that R. N. Elliott developed his wave methodology through contemplation of Dow Theory.[7] Richard W. Schabacker, Robert D. Edwards, and John Magee also recognized Dow Theory as seminal to their thinking, with Edwards and Magee's book *Technical Analysis of Stock Trends*, for example, devoting three chapters to the subject.

Indeed, *Technical Analysis of Stock Trends*, first printed in 1948, as well as its predecessors, Schabacker's *Technical Analysis and Stock Market Profits*, from 1932, and *Profits in the Stock Market*, by Harold M. Gartley in 1935, are milestones in the development of trend following methodology. Given the focus in these books on technical patterns such as flags, pennants, triangles, head-and-shoulders patterns, etc., it may seem peculiar to associate these books with trend following, but the point behind being able to distinguish such patterns is precisely to recognize signals for trend beginnings, continuations, and ends. To quote from Edwards: "Profits are made by capitalizing on up or down trends, by following them until they are reversed."[8]

Aha! The terms "trends" and "following" separated by only the space of a word, suggestive of an underlying trading philosophy supporting the myriad of details.

The second book, by William D. Gann titled *Truth of the Stock Tape*, first published in 1923, also emphasizes the trend: "The way to make money is to determine the trend and then follow it."[9] Indeed, the focus in this book, and other works of Gann's that followed, was, in one way or another, to take trades in the direction of the market's trend. Perhaps to the surprise of some, *Truth of the Stock Tape* is a very conventional work, given Gann's later reputation for esotericism and astrology.

The third book was Richard D. Wyckoff's *Studies in Tape Reading*, published in 1910. Significantly, Wyckoff uses the term "follow the trend" (albeit in a short term, day trading context) when discussing one Jacob Field, "Prince of the Floor Traders," but he does not follow through with a philosophy or description.[10]

A few years later, however, Wyckoff was more decisively on the side of trend following, actually publishing a newsletter titled the *Trend Letter*. In a similar vein, in a later work, Wyckoff uses an interesting metaphor for trend following: "A small trader should be a hitch-hiker."[11] But with respect to using charts as a means for profitably trading the markets, Wyckoff was skeptical:

> "Let anyone who thinks he can make money following a Figure Chart or any other kind of chart have a friend prepare it, keeping secret the name of the stock and the period covered. Then put down on paper a positive set of rules which are to be strictly adhered to, so

that there can be no guesswork. Each situation will then call for a certain play and no deviation is to be allowed. Cover up with a sheet of paper all but the beginning of the chart, gradually sliding the paper to the right as you progress. Record each order and execution just as if actually trading. Put Rollo Tape down as coppering every trade and when done send him a check for what you have lost."[12]

Of course, the methodology suggested by Wyckoff can now routinely be done on an iterative basis by computer. Not one, but millions of tests can be done with a rapidity that would have astonished Wyckoff. But would his judgment have changed? Possibly, since many years later, Wyckoff was using charts to draw trendlines, or as he called them, supply lines and demand lines, depending upon whether these lines connected high or low points.

Let us get back to practice again, and return to Jesse Livermore, who communicated much about his trading, either through Lefèvre's articles, or through a book he wrote himself in 1940, *How to Trade in Stocks*. The early Livermore can be considered to have been at least partially a trend follower inasmuch as he began his trading program in a small way at first, only "adding to his line" if the market went in his direction, and abandoning it otherwise (essentially the advice of Dickson Watts in 1891). He was also apparently a "breakout" trader, at one point describing a stock that was bouncing back and forth between two price levels, but observing that eventually either buying or selling would become stronger, and "the price will break through the old barrier."[13]

This breakout, then, would define the "line of least resistance." Later, he says, "Well, when the price line of least resistance is established I follow it."[14]

Going forward to 1940 Livermore can more definitely be considered to have been a trend follower in that, in *How to Trade in Stocks*, he advocated the use of specific buy and sell signals based on his analysis of the perceived trend. At one point, Livermore uses the term "following the trend" directly: "It may surprise many to know that in my method of trading, when I see by my records that an upward trend is in progress, I become a buyer as soon as a stock makes a new high on its movement, after having had a normal reaction. The same applies whenever I take the short side. Why? Because I am following the trend at the time. My records signal me to go ahead!"[15]

Note that the verb "follow" has become the present participle "following"—an important conceptual necessity (though not the final one), I believe, in solidifying the idea of trend following as a continuing or recurring action.

Central to Livermore's philosophy was the recording of "pivotal points," or intermediate highs and lows. These "pivotal points" were in part the same thing as Dow Theory intermediate highs and lows, or Edwards and Magee's "basing points." Initiation and liquidation signals were based on significant movement away from these pivotal points—either three or six points, depending upon the type of rally or reaction that was being considered, for a stock selling above $30. Thus, Livermore's formula was not a breakout system, nor a trendline system, but rather a type of "filter rule," though a bit more complicated than the typically tested sort. The parameters used were arbitrary, but according to Livermore, based on much experience. Today you can optimize parameters by computer to save time.

Livermore's method certainly has some appeal, but one cannot help thinking that it might have been better understood and traded if it were chart based. But Livermore was not a chartist: "Personally, charts have never appealed to me. I think they are altogether too confusing."[16]

In addition to the work of Edwards, Magee, Livermore, and the others, the 1930s and 1940s saw several other advances relating to the theory and evidence for trend following. One of the more interesting studies came from the Cowles Commission for Economic Research (now the Cowles Foundation at Yale University) in 1937. Written by Alfred Cowles III (founder of the institution) and Herbert E. Jones, this study investigated the probabilities of sequences of rises and falls in stock market prices over several time horizons, ranging from 20 minutes to seven months. Its conclusion was that, yes, there was a tendency for the market to continue in the same direction as the period before. In short, there was serial correlation: At least from one period to the next, there was trendiness, and some justification for the use of trading methodologies that might today be called trend following. In summary, the study states:

> "This evidence of structure in stock prices suggests alluring possibilities in the way of forecasting. In fact, many professional speculators, including in particular exponents of the so-called 'Dow Theory' widely publicized by popular financial journals, have adopted systems based in the main on the principle that it is advantageous to swim with the tide."[17]

Also worthy of note was a 1949 article in *Fortune*, "Fashions in Forecasting," by Alfred Winslow Jones (yes, that Alfred Winslow Jones—originator of the hedge fund concept and founder of the first hedge fund). In the article, Jones analyzes many of the then-current stock forecasting techniques, such as Mansfield Mills' buying and selling curves, Dow Theory, and other methods having trend following characteristics. His explanation of trend following revolves around acceptance of "the undoubted fact of momentum in psychological trends." The process he describes sounds something like George Soros's reflexivity:

"Thus a movement of the stock market once under way generates unrealistic optimism or pessimism, so that the trend of prices then carries through and beyond some point of central value. After that, turned by profit takers or bargain hunters, with the basic forces of supply and demand altered, the market pendulum starts back and passes again through and beyond a point of reasonable value, wherever it may be. Therefore, the chances are worth considering that once a trend has reversed itself to some measured extent (as determined by the Dow Theory, or by the penetration of a moving average or trend line), the new trend will continue far enough to make it worth following."[18]

It is notable that Jones uses the exact terms "trend followers" and "trend following" in his article. But the meaning of the words perhaps differs from its usage today. For example, when he states that "what Mills and Lowry have are still trend following tools, with all their advantages and limitations," he seems to mean something more like "trend-lagging"—such as when a moving average turns higher after a trend has already begun. In other words, trend following was not yet a fully formed concept. "Trend" was not yet a noun adjunct, nor "following" a gerund.

The individual who finally made the connection was perhaps William Dunnigan, a trader, technical analyst, and writer who ran a business cycle forecasting company in Palo Alto, California, in the 1950s. Dunnigan had many books and other publications to his credit, beginning with the academic *Forecasting the Monthly Movement of Stock Prices* in 1930, and following with a more technically oriented, mimeographed publication called "Trading With the Trend" in 1934, to name two. His major works, however, came out in the early and mid 1950s.

Dunnigan is perhaps best known today for his "thrust" methodologies and "one way" system; but his overall market perceptions were broad and deep. He had a knack for verbal innovation, including the invention of terms such as "trap forecasting" and "continuous forecasting," used to distinguish between those trades designed to capture quick profits ("catching the market in a trap") and those with an indefinite duration whose exit levels were determined on a day-to-day basis, depending on market action. Starting with these perceptions, the transition to "trend following" is not an arduous one, for if a market is "trapped" into a directional commitment at the point of, say, a breakout (i.e., it generates a "signal"), then "continuous forecasting" takes over until the next "trap" (to liquidate or perhaps reverse) is signaled. But, if that is the model, then is the "forecasting" part of the formulation really necessary? Is not the process rather one of monitoring the market for the occurrence of the next "trap," and then, when it occurs, acting upon it?

Ultimately, in his 1954 work *New Blueprints for Gains in Stocks and Grains,* that is what Dunnigan concluded, giving us some of the earliest articulated insights into the philosophy behind trend following:

> "We think that forecasting should be thought of in the light of measuring the direction of today's trend and then turning to the Law of Inertia (momentum) for assurance that probabilities favor the continuation of that trend for an unknown period of time into the future. This is trend following, and it does not require us to don the garment of the mystic and look into the crystal balls of the future."[19]

And again:

> "Let us believe that it is possible to profit through economic changes by following today's trend, as it is revealed statistically day-by-day, week-by-week, or month-by-month. In doing this we should entertain no preconceived notions as to whether business is going to boom or bust, or whether the Dow-Jones Industrial Average is going to 500 or 50. We will merely chart our course and steer our ship in the direction of the prevailing wind. When the economic weather changes, we will change our course with it and will not try to forecast the future time or place at which the wind will change."[20]

William Dunnigan today remains an underrated trading researcher, although he was highly, if not widely, regarded in his day, even by academic economists. Elmer Clark Bratt, for example, refers to Dunnigan's "trading with the trend" in his *Business Cycles and Forecasting,* one of the premier economics textbooks of his day:

> "Intermediate movements in the stock market do not last any stated length of time, so we never know just when a rally or a reaction will take place. What has been called "trading with the trend" by Dunnigan appears to be the only important forecasting principle which can be derived."[21]

Next in line among the pioneers of trend following was the much better known Richard Donchian, whose article "Trend-Following Methods in Commodity Price Analysis" appeared in the *Commodity Yearbook* of 1957. Donchian's article was written in a confident, matter-of-fact manner suggesting that he had a long, intimate knowledge of the principles about which he wrote, particularly the use of moving averages and "swing trading," both developed in the article as examples of trend following methodology. Like Dunnigan, Donchian discussed more than just the trading systems themselves; he also discussed the philosophy behind them. The comments he made about trend following still hold true:

"Every good trend-following method should automatically limit the loss on any position, long or short, without limiting the gain. Whenever a trend, once established, reverses quickly, there is always a point, not far above or below the extreme reached prior to the reversal, at which evidence of a trend in the opposite direction is given. At that point any position held in the direction of the original trend should be reversed—or at least closed out—at a limited loss. Profits are not limited because whenever a trend, once established, continues in a sustained fashion without giving any evidence of trend reversal, the trend-following principle requires that a market position be maintained as long as the trend continues."[22]

Richard Donchian, as most traders are aware, did much more than write about trend following. He was also a broker, analyst, and trader, who most significantly was the founder of the first publicly managed futures fund, the moving average–based Futures, Inc., in 1948.[23]

Starting in 1960, he began writing a weekly commodity "Trend Timing" letter, based on one of his better-known trend following systems, the 5-20 moving average method, thereby creating a documented decades-long performance record for his trading methodology. Further, Donchian was an innovator in advancing an idea that is now the norm among large futures trading entities everywhere—the concept of trading many markets at the same time in a portfolio:

"When I first got into commodities, no one was interested in a diversified approach. There were cocoa men, cotton men, grain men…they were worlds apart. I was almost the first one who decided to look at all commodities together. Nobody before had looked at the whole picture and had taken a diversified position with the idea of cutting losses short and going with a trend."[24]

And so with Dunnigan and Donchian the story comes to an end. Although these two were by no means the first trend followers, nor surely the last, they were truly a watershed in the history of trend following. While many of the ideas that preceded theirs were trend following in nature, they were largely inchoate, with an unstated or incomplete underlying philosophy. Dunnigan and Donchian, however, articulated this philosophy—indeed, called it trend following—and thereby laid a foundation upon which later methodologies could comfortably rest. The narrative continues, of course, but since it has already been well and amply covered, I will stop at this point. Suffice it to say, however, that everyone remains under the influence of these pioneers of trend following, whether people know it or not.

You can read an unabridged version of Stig Ostgaard's, "On the Nature and Origins of Trend Following" at www.trendfollowing.com/resources.html.

It's quite true what philosophy
says, that life must be
understood backwards.
But one then forgets the other
principle, that it must be lived
forwards. A principle which,
the more one thinks it through,
precisely leads to the conclusion
that life in time can never be
properly understood, just
because no moment can acquire
the complete stillness needed to
orient oneself backward.[25]

Carl Sagan didn't want
to believe.
He wanted to **know**.

Cheat Sheet

Author Seth Godin said it well: "Golf is not safe. My grandfather died playing golf. Speaking up is not safe. People might be offended. Innovation is not safe. You'll fail. Perhaps badly. Now that we've got that out of the way, what are you going to do about it? Hide? Crouch in a corner and work as hard as you can to fit in? That's not safe, either. Might as well do something that matters instead."[1]

I live and breathe my research firm. Reaching and teaching people my lessons is rewarding. Take advantage of my work, and you will either make or save a great deal of money. For your associates, friends, and family—some bullet point ways to describe and explain systematic trend following trading:

- **Profit in up and down markets:** Trend following doesn't swear an allegiance to a bull or bear market. It follows trends to the end. No matter how ridiculous trends might appear early and no matter how insanely extended they might appear at the end, follow trends. Why? They always go farther than anyone expects. Ignore momentum at your peril.

- **No more buy and hold, analysts, or news:** Trend following decision-making doesn't involve discretion, guesses, gut feelings, or hunches. It's not day trading or buy and hope. It doesn't involve passive indexing, in and out trading, or fundamental analysis. No more 24-hour news cycles, daily turbulence, or sensational hype. No black boxes or magic formulas either. Let go of the Holy Grails.

- **No prediction:** Trends exist everywhere, always coming and always going. Markets are no different: They trend up and down. That said, no one can predict a market trend, you can only react to one. Trend following never anticipates the beginning or end of a trend. It only acts when the trend changes. There is no need to figure out why a market is trending, just follow it. You don't need to understand electricity to use it.

- **The big money of letting profits run:** Trend following at its best aims to compound absolute returns. It doesn't shoot for average. The goal is to make the knock your socks off returns, not passbook savings interest. Trend following also has the unique ability to lie and wait for targets of opportunity. That means making a killing on unpredictable surprises.

- **Risk management is top priority:** Trend following always has defined exit protocols to control injury to your account. Stop losses and proper leverage usage are standard practice. Trend following also has low to negative correlations with most other investment opportunities.

- **Takes advantage of mass psychology:** Trend following takes advantage of panicky sheep behavior. Strict discipline minimizes behavioral biases. It solves the eagerness to realize gains and reluctance to crystallize losses. Too many people believe what pleases them. Most behaviors are simply driven by the impulsive moment of *now*. Trend following wins because of that.

- **Scientific approach to trading:** Trend following doesn't require a belief, but rather it relies on unwavering scientific principles. It has a defined edge just like the MIT card-counting team that beat Vegas casinos. Be the casino, not the hapless player. Trend following uses rigid rules rooted in numbers. Think process not outcome. Remember, frequency of correctness is not the issue, the magnitude of correctness matters. Winning percentage means zilch.

- **Strong historical performance in crisis periods:** Trend following is adaptable to differing climates and environments performing best during periods of rising volatility and uncertainty. The unknown will happen again. Are you ready? You have to be able to ride the bucking bronco. Ride out the storm and stay alive.

- **No traditional diversification:** Trend following is not restricted to any single market or instrument. A focus on price action allows trend following to be applied to an exceptionally large variety of markets. Price is the one thing that all markets have in common. A trend trading system for Treasury Bonds should also work on the Euro and stocks. Trend following is robust.

> The most important shot in golf is the next one.[2]

- **No government reliance:** Forget Social Security, bailouts, stimulus plans, and roads to nowhere. Those won't help you to make money; they only help you lose. When the Fed puts on or takes off the training wheels (read: rate manipulation), will you be ready to mint cash or will you sit there and just take it again? If your portfolio is grounded in sound principles, you can win no matter what happens.

Q. Do you expect to make money in both good markets and bad?

A. There are not good or bad markets. There are up or down markets.

Quick Commandments

The great trend following traders have been motivated by possibility and opportunity, unlike crowds
of panicky sheep unwilling or unable to leave the
herd. Great trend traders seek options, experiences,
choices, and paths. They never quit or allow themselves to be muddled by the latest fashion.

> Teach us to care and
> not to care. Teach
> us to sit still.[1]

In that spirit, these are some of my favorite money-making gems pulled
from the historical wisdom of trend trading pioneers Richard Donchian,
William Dunnigan, Amos Hostetter, Jesse Livermore, Roy Longstreet, and
Dickson Watts:

- Don't fight the tape!
- Like sharp instruments and strong spirits, leverage confers many bene-
  fits, but only when used with care.
- Limit losses and ride profits, irrespective of all other rules.
- Of all the speculative blunders, there are few greater than trying to
  average a losing game.
- Always sell what shows you a loss and keep what shows you a profit.
- You can't force a market into giving you something it doesn't have to
  give.
- Talk is cheap and rumors are even cheaper.
- Courage in a speculator is merely the confidence to act on the decision
  of his mind.
- A loss never bothers me after I take it. But being wrong, not taking the
  loss, that is what does the damage to the pocketbook and to the soul.
- The trend is evident to a man who has an open mind and reasonably
  clear sight.
- In a narrow market, when price moves within a narrow range, the thing
  to do is to watch the market, read the tape to determine the limits of
  prices, and make up your mind that you will not take an interest until
  the price breaks through the limit in either direction.
- Watch the market with one objective: to determine the direction of
  price tendency.
- Prices, like everything else, move along the line of least resistance.

- It cost me a million dollars to learn that the dangerous enemy to a trader is the susceptibility to the urging of magnetic personality combined with a brilliant mind.
- Have a profit? Forget it. Have a loss? Forget it even quicker.
- It was never my thinking that made the big money for me. It was my sitting, my sitting tight.
- There is only one side to the stock market and it is not the bull side or the bear side, but the right side.
- If you don't know what's going on, don't do anything.
- Markets are never wrong, opinions often are.
- Don't be too curious about the reasons behind moves.
- The smarter you are, the longer it takes.
- When time is up, markets will reverse.
- Don't expect the tape to be a lecturer. It's enough to see that something is wrong.
- Don't imagine that a market that once sold at 150 is cheap at 130.
- A man does not swear eternal allegiance to either the bear or bull side.
- People believe what it pleases them to believe.
- Trend followers plan when they will get out before they ever get in.
- Know every day what your portfolio is worth.
- Calculate what your risks are on any given day for all positions.
- Controlling risk is not the same thing as avoiding risk. If managing risk is an integral part of your philosophy, when your risk level goes up or down, you simply adjust.
- Buy market strength and sell market weakness.
- Keep a positive attitude, no matter how much you lose.
- Don't take the market home.
- Dream big dreams and think tall. Very few people set goals too high. A man becomes what he thinks about all day long.
- In the world of money, in a world shaped by human behavior, nobody has the foggiest notion of what will happen in the future. Mark that word. Nobody.
- When the ship starts to sink, don't pray...jump!
- Assimilate into your very bones a set of trading rules that works for you.
- Thou shall not trade against the trend up or down.
- There is nothing new on Wall Street. There can't be, because speculation is as old as the hills.

- Whatever happens in the stock market today has happened before and will happen again.
- Sell when you can, not when you have to.
- An ability to shift on a dime is critical when shifting time comes.
- A common deception—self-deception.
- Fools try to prove that they are right. Wise men try to find when they are wrong.
- All see; few observe, fewer still compare.
- The foolishness of the many is the opportunity of the few.
- The man who conforms never transforms.
- When you begin to doubt, begin to get out.
- Make believe is a game society plays as well as children.
- Some men are alive after they are dead; others are dead while still alive.
- It's not about how much can you make, but how much can you lose.
- The unpardonable sin—not to make money.

Lastly, consider William Worthington Fowler's wisdom circa 1870: "To the merchant and banker, it is a financial centre, collecting and distributing money, regulating the exchanges of a continent and striking balances of trade with London and Frankfort. To the outside observer and novice, it is a kind of work-shop thronged by cunning artisans who work in precious metals, where vessels of gold and silver are wrought or made to shine with fresh luster, and where old china is fire-gilt as good as new. The moralist and philosopher look upon it as a gambling-den, a cage of unclean birds, an abomination where men drive a horrible trade, fattening and battening on the substance of their friends and neighbors—or perhaps a kind of modern coliseum where gladiatorial combats are joined, and bulls, bears, and other ferocious beasts gore and tear each other for public amusement. The brokers regard it as a place of business where, in mercantile parlance, they may ply a legitimate trade, buying and selling for others on commission. To the speculators, it is a caravansera where they may load or unload their camels and drive them away betimes to some pleasant oasis. To the financial commanders it is an arsenal in which their arms and chariots are stored, the stronghold to be defended or besieged, the field for strategy, battles and plunder."

> Some mistakes you never stop paying for.[2]

Note: Shout to Ritholtz.com for the Fowler find.

Bibliography

Angus, Jeff. *Management by Baseball: The Official Rules for Winning Management in Any Field.* New York: Harper Collins Publishers, 2006.

Basso, Thomas. *Panic-Proof Investing: Lessons in Profitable Investing from a Market Wizard.* Hoboken: John Wiley and Sons, Inc., 1994.

Bernstein, Peter, and Annalyn Swan. *All the Money in the World: How the Forbes 400 Make—and Spend—Their Fortunes.* New York: Alfred A. Knopf, 2007.

Bernstein, Peter. *Against the Gods: The Remarkable Story of Risk.* New York: John Wiley and Sons, Inc., 1996.

Brogen, Chris, and Julien Smith. *Trust Agents: Using the Web to Build Influence, Improve Reputation, and Earn Trust.* Hoboken: John Wiley and Sons, Inc., 2009.

Brown, Kedrick. *Trend Trading: Timing Market Tides.* Hoboken: John Wiley and Sons, Inc., 2006.

Christie, Ian, ed. *Gilliam on Gilliam.* New York, NY: Faber and Faber Ltd., 1999.

Collins, Art. *Market Beaters.* Greenville: Traders Press Inc., 2004.

Colvin, Geoff. *Talent Is Overrated: What Really Separates World-Class Performers from Everybody Else.* New York: Penguin Group, 2008.

Covel, Michael. *The Complete TurtleTrader: The Legend, the Lessons, the Results.* New York: Harper Collins, 2007.

Covel, Michael. *Trend Following: Learn to Make Millions in Up or Down Markets.* Upper Saddle River: Pearson Education, 2009.

Coyle, Daniel. *The Talent Code: Greatness Isn't Born. It's Grown. Here's How.* New York: Bantam Books, 2009.

Crabel, Toby. *Day Trading with Short Term Price Patterns and Opening Range Breakout.* Jupiter: Rahfelt and Associates, 1990.

Douglas, Mark. *The Disciplined Trader: Developing Winning Attitudes.* New York: New York Institute of Finance, 1990.

Dubner, Stephen, and Steven D. Levitt. *Freakonomics: A Rogue Economist Explores the Hidden Side of Everything.* New York: Harper Collins, 2005.

Eng, William. *Trading Rules: Strategies for Success.* Chicago: Dearborn Financial Publishing, Inc., 1990.

Fabricand, Burton. *The Science of Winning: A Random Walk Along the Road to Investment Riches.* London: High Stakes Publishing, 2002.

Farleigh, Richard. *Taming the Lion: 100 Secret Strategies for Investing.* Great Britain: Harriman House Publishing, 2005.

Fried, Jason, and David Heinemeier. *Rework.* New York: Crown Publishing Group, 2010.

Friedman, Thomas L. *Hot, Flat, and Crowded: Why We Need a Green Revolution—And How It Can Renew America.* New York: Farrar, Straus, and Giroux, 2008.

Friedman, Thomas L. *The Lexus and the Olive Tree.* New York: Farrar, Straus, and Giroux, 1999.

Geisst, Charles. *100 Years of Wall Street.* New York: McGraw Hill, 2000.

Gladwell, Malcolm. *The Tipping Point: How Little Things Can Make a Big Difference.* New York: Little, Brown and Company, 2000.

Godin, Seth. *Linchpin.* New York: Penguin Group, 2010.

Goleman, Daniel. *Emotional Intelligence: Why it can matter more than IQ.* New York: Bantam Books, 1995.

James, Bill. *The New Bill James Historical Baseball Abstract.* New York: The Free Press, 2001.

Kacher, Chris, and Gil Morales. *Trade Like an O'Neil Disciple: How we made 18,000% in the Stock Market.* Hoboken: John Wiley and Sons, Inc., 2010.

Kaufman, Perry. *Smarter Trading: Improving Performance in Changing Markets.* New York: McGraw Hill, Inc., 1995.

Kaufman, Perry. *Trading Systems and Methods.* Hoboken: John Wiley and Sons, 1998.

Kawaski, Guy. *The Art of the Start.* New York: Penguin Group, 2004.

Keyes, Franklin C. *Wall Street Speculation: Its Tricks and Its Tragedies.* Burlington: Fraser Publishing Company, 1904.

Kleinfield, Sonny. *The Traders.* Greenfield: Holt, Rinehart, and Winston, 1993.

Koppel, Robert. *The Intuitive Trader: Developing Your Inner Trading Wisdom.* Hoboken: John Wiley and Sons, Inc., 1996.

Koy, Kevin. *The Big Hitters: Interviews with the World's Foremost Market Movers.* Chicago: Intermarket Publishing Corp., 1986.

Kroll, Stanley. *The Professional Commodity Trader.* Greenville: Traders Press Incorporated, 1974.

Le Beau, Charles, and David W. Lucas. *Technical Traders Guide to Computer Analysis of the Futures Market.* Homewood: Business One Irwin, 1992.

Lewis, Michael. *The Art of Winning an Unfair Game.* New York: W.W. Norton and Company, Inc., 2003.

Livermore, Jesse. *How to Trade in Stocks: The Livermore Formula for Combining Time Element and Price.* Rahway: Quinn and Boden Company, 1940.

Livingston, Jessica. *Founders at Work: Stories of Startups' Early Days.* New York: Apress, 2008.

Loeb, G. M. *The Battle for Investment Survival.* New York: Simon and Schuster, 1957.

Longstreet, Roy. *Viewpoints of a Commodity Trader.* Greenville: Traders Press, 1967.

Mallaby, Sebastian. *More Money than God: Hedge Funds and the Making of a New Elite.* New York: The Penguin Press, 2010.

Mauboussin, Michael. *More Than You Know: Finding Financial Wisdom in Unconventional Places.* New York: Columbia Business School, 2006.

Narang, Rishi. *Inside the Black Box: The Simple Truth About Quantitative Trading.* Hoboken: John Wiley and Sons, Inc., 2009.

Neill, Humphrey. *Tape Reading: Market and Tactics.* LaVergne: BN Publishing, 2008.

O'Shaughnessy, James. *What Works on Wall Street: A Guide to the Best-Performing Investment Strategies of all Time.* New York: McGraw Hill, 1997.

Patel, Charles. *Technical Trading Systems for Commodities and Stocks.* Greenville: Traders Press, Inc., 1998.

Paulos, John Allen. *A Mathematician Plays the Stock Market.* New York: Perseus Book Group, 2003.

Peltz, Louis. *The New Investment Superstars: 13 Great Investors and Their Strategies for Superior Returns.* Hoboken: John Wiley and Sons, Inc., 2001.

Poundstone, William. *Fortune's Formula: The Untold Story of the Scientific Betting System That Beat the Casinos and Wall Street.* New York: Hill and Wang, 2005.

Ritholtz, Barry, and Aaron Task. *Bailout Nation.* Hoboken: John Wiley and Sons, Inc., 2009.

Rodgers, Jim. *Investment Biker: On the Road With Jim Rogers.* New York: Random House, Inc., 1994.

Rosenblum, Irwin. *Up, Down, Up, Down, Up: My Career at Commodities Corporation.* United States: Xlibris, 2003.

Schroeder, Alice. *The Snowball: Warren Buffett and the Business of Life.* New York: Bantam Books, 2008.

Schwager, Jack D. *Market Wizards: Interviews with Top Traders.* Columbia: Marketplace Books, 2006.

Stridsman, Thomas. *Trading Systems That Work: Building and Evaluating Effective Trading Systems.* New York: McGraw Hill, 2001.

Taleb, Nassim Nicholas. *Fooled By Randomness: The Hidden Role of Chance in the Markets and in Life.* New York: TEXERE, 2001.

Taleb, Nassim Nicholas. *The Black Swan: The Impact of the Highly Improbable.* New York: The Random House Publishing Group, 2007.

Taleb, Nassim. *The Bed of Procrustes: Philosophical and Practical Aphorisms.* New York: Random House Publishing Group, 2010.

Tharp, Van. *Trade Your Way to Financial Freedom.* New York: McGraw Hill, Inc., 2007.

Thomas, Conrad W. *Risk and Opportunity: A New Approach to Stock Market Profits.* Homewood: Dow Jones-Irwin, Inc., 1974.

"The Trader." *Commonsense Speculation.* Burlington: Fraser Publishing Company, 1992.

Von Mises, Ludwig. *Human Action: A Treatise on Economics, Fourth Edition.* Irvington-on-Hudson: The Foundation for Economic Education, Inc., 1996.

Watts, Dickson G. *Speculation as a Fine Art: And Thoughts on Life.* New York: Traders Press, 1965.

Wilkinson, Chris. *Technically Speaking: Tips and Strategies from 16 Top Analysts.* Greenville: Traders Press, Inc., 1997.

The Winton Papers. London: Winton Capital Management Ltd., 2003.

Woods Jr., Thomas. *Meltdown: A Free-Market Look at Why the Stock Market Collapsed, the Economy Tanked, and Government Bailouts Will Make Things Worse.* Washington, DC: Regnery Publishing, Inc., 2009.

Zuckerman, Gregory. *The Greatest Trade Ever: The Behind-the-Scenes Story of How John Paulson Defied Wall Street and Made Financial History.* New York: Random House, Inc., 2009.

Endnotes

Contents

1. *The Matrix*, dir. Andy and Larry Wachowski, perf. Laurence Fishburne, DVD, Warner Bros. Pictures, 1999.

Ignition

1. Epictetus, Greek philosopher.

2. Smashing Pumpkins, "Bullet with Butterfly Wings." *Mellon Collie and the Infinite Sadness*, Virgin Records, October 24, 1995.

3. Stan Grossfeld, "Plane talk with Sox higher-ups." November 5, 2010. See http://www.boston.com/sports/baseball/redsox/articles/2010/11/05/plane_talk_with_sox_higher_ups.

4. Jason Fried and David Heinemeier, *Rework*. New York: Crown Publishing Group, 2010, p. 142.

5. Seth Godin blog post, "Hourly Work vs. Linchpin Work." June 9, 2010. See http://sethgodin.typepad.com/seths_blog/2010/06/hourly-work-vs-linchpin-work.html.

Expectations

1. Chinese proverb.

2. John Mills, *On Credit Cycles and the Origin of Commercial Panic*. Manchester: Manchester Statistical Society, 1867.

3. Kent Thune, "Naive Science and the Nature of Financial Markets." February 2, 2011. See http://www.thefinancialphilosopher.com/2011/02/understanding-markets-nature-not-naivety-or-narcissism.html.

Jargon

1. Henry Ford.

2. See http://www.foxbusiness.com/personal-finance/2011/04/05/questionable-investment.

Show Me the Money

1. *Willy Wonka and the Chocolate Factory*, dir. Mel Stuart, perf. Gene Wilder, VHS, Warner Bros., 1971.

2. See http://www.forbes.com/profile/bruce-kovner.

3. Francis Storrs, "The 50 Wealthiest Bostonians." *Boston Magazine*, May 15, 2006. See http://www.bostonmagazine.com/articles/the_50_wealthiest_bostonians/.

4. Dr. Steve Sjuggerud, "How to Make $80 Million in a Brutal Bear Market." *Daily Wealth*, April 11, 2009. See http://www.Dailywealth.com.

5. Martin Schwartz, *Pit Bull: Lessons from Wall Street's Champion Day Trader*. New York: Harper Collins, 1999.

6. See http://en.wikipedia.org/wiki/David_Harding (mathematician).

7. Jack D. Schwager, *Market Wizards*. New York: NYIF Corp., 1989.

8. See http://www.absolutereturn-alpha.com.

9. Jack D. Schwager, *The New Market Wizards*. New York: HarperBusiness, 1992.

10. See http://www.forbes.com/profile/louis-bacon.

11. See http://www.forbes.com/profile/paul-tudor-jones.

12. Man Group front page, March 23, 2011. See http://www.mangroupplc.com/.

13. 2008 Sunrise Capital Chart.

14. 2009 Sunrise Capital Chart.

15. 2010 Sunrise Capital Chart.

16. Mulvaney Capital Management: Global Diversified Program. See http://www.mulvaneycapital.com.

17. Albert Einstein.

18. Michael Covel, *Trend Following: Learn to Make Millions in Up or Down Markets*. Upper Saddle River, New Jersey: Pearson Education, 2009, p. 230.

19. Jim Rogers, *Investment Biker*. New York: Random House, 1994.

Blowing Bubbles

1. Pink Floyd, "Comfortably Numb." *The Wall*, writer Roger Waters, EMI, 1979.

2. Sally Hogshead, *Fascinate: Your 7 Triggers to Persuasion and Captivation*. New York: Harper Collins, 2010, p. 117.

3. "Mind Over Money: Can Markets Be Rational When Humans Are Not?" NOVA, April 26, 2010.

4. Ibid.

5. Ibid.

6. Ibid.

7. Ibid.

8. Ibid.

9. James Montier, "Mind Matters: Forever Blowing Bubbles: Moral Hazard and Melt-up." *Societe Generale*, June 2, 2009.

10. "The Monsters Are Due on Maple Street." *The Twilight Zone*, March 4, 1960.

11. Barry Ritholtz, "Why politics and investing don't mix." *Washington Post*, February 6, 2011.

Speculari

1. *Wall Street: Money Never Sleeps*, dir. Oliver Stone, perf. Michael Douglas, DVD, 20th Century Fox, 2010.

2. *Wall Street*, dir. Oliver Stone, perf. Michael Douglas, DVD, 20th Century Fox, 1987.

3. *The Winton Papers*. See http://www.wintoncapital.com.

4. Todd Miller, Blog post responding to the *Winton Papers*, November 6, 2010. See http://www.michaelcovel.com/2010/11/06/the-winton-papers-speculation-wise/.

5. Dickson Watts, *Speculation as a Fine Art*. New York: Traders Press, 1965.

6. Jeffrey A. Tucker, "Work for Free." July 5, 2010. See http://mises.org/daily/4547.

Fundamentals Are Religion

1. Joseph Brean, "A day in the intellectual glare of Hitchens: Contrarian opines on religion to his crowd of followers." Canadian *National Post*, November 18, 2006.

2. *Financial Trader*, Vol. 1, No. 7. September/October 1994, 26.2.

3. "The History of the Motley Fool." Fool.com, November 4, 2003. See http://www.fool.com.

4. Michael Gibbons. See http://gibbonstrading.com/analysis.htm.

5. Covel, *Trend Following*, p. 90.

6. Stephen Taub, "Paul Tudor Jones II." June 30, 2008. See http://www.absolutereturn-alpha.com/Article/1964189/Paul-Tudor-Jones-II.html.

7. Blog post response to "Aunt May's Arthritis Cure; No Need to Add to Trend Following." February 7, 2011. See http://www.michaelcovel.com/2011/02/06/aunt-mays-arthritis-cure-no-need-to-add-to-trend-following/.

Everything Flows

1. Nassim Taleb, *The Bed of Procrustes: Philosophical and Practical Aphorisms*. New York: Random House, 2010, p. 80.

2. See http://www.seykota.com.

3. See http://www.seykota.com.

4. See http://www.gibbonstrading.com.

Systematic Trend Following

1. Van K. Tharp, *Trade Your Way to Financial Freedom*. New York: McGraw-Hill, 1999.

2. Jim Simons. See http://www.hedgeworld.com.

3. Daniel P. Collins in *Futures*, October 2003.

4. Cullen Roche, "The Market is a Heartless Beast." January 2011. See http://pragcap.com/the-market-is-a-heartless-beast.

5. John P. Hussman, Ph.D., "Overvalued, Overbought, Overbullish, and Rising Yields." January 12, 2011. See http://investmentwatchblog.com/overvalued-overbought-over-bullish-and-rising-yields/.

6. Michael Gibbons. See http://www.gibbonstrading.com.

7. Sebastian Mallaby, *More Money than God*. New York: Penguin Press, 2010.

Change

1. *Bruce Lee: A Warrior's Journey*, dir. John Little and Bruce Lee, perf. Bruce Lee, Warner Home Video, DVD, October 22, 2000.

2. John W. Henry. Presentation in Geneva, Switzerland, September 15, 1998.

3. Thomas Friedman, *The Lexus and the Olive Tree*. New York: Farrar, Straus, and Giroux, 1999.

4. Mary Ann Burns, "Industry Icons Assess the Managed Futures Business." Futures Industry Association (May/June 2003).

5. J. P. Morgan.

No Prediction

1. Eric Schmidt's speech, Abu Dhabi Media Summit, March 2010.

2. Mark S. Rzepczynski, "John W. Henry & Co. Year in Review." December 2000.

3. Covel, *Trend Following*, p. 49.

4. E-mail to http://www.turtletrader.com.

Price Action

1. *Miller's Crossing*, dir. Joel Coen, DVD, 20th Century Fox, 1990.

2. From Upstairs/Downstairs Seminar with Tom Baldwin and Peter Borish. Futures Industry Association, 1994.

3. Covel, *Trend Following*, p. 18.

4. Michael Gibbons, "Eight Trading Basics and Rules." See http://www.gibbonstrading.com/trading.htm.

5. Kevin Koy, *The Big Hitters*. Chicago: Intermarket Publishing Corp., 1986.

Place Your Bet

1. Archimedes, Greek astronomer, mathematician, physicist, engineer, and inventor.

2. Commencement address given before the graduating class of 1989, University of Georgia, June 17, 1989.

3. Larry Hite.

Trading Systems

1. *The Blues Brothers*, dir. John Landis, DVD, Universal Studios, June 20, 1980.

2. Charles Faulkner, "Inside the Counterintuitive World of Trend Followers: It's Not What You Think. It's What You Know." *SFO Magazine,* April 2005.

3. "William Eckhardt: Top Systems Traders." Futures Industry Association. Speech on audiotape, 1992.

4. James Simons, "Mathematics, Common Sense, and Good Luck." Greenwich Roundtable, June 17, 1999.

5. See http://www.altispartners.com.

6. Ibid.

7. Ibid.

8. Ed Seykota. See http://www.seykota.com.

9. Gibbons Burke, "Managing Your Money." *Active Trader,* July 2000.

10. Craig Pauley, "How to Become a CTA." Based on Chicago Mercantile Exchange Seminars, 1992–1994. June 1994.

11. Ed Seykota and Dave Druz, "Determining Optimal Risk." *Technical Analysis of Stocks and Commodities Magazine,* Vol. 11, No. 3, March 1993, 122–124. See http://www.traders.com.

12. Francais Vaca quoted in CTA Confidential, "An Ongoing Series of Qualitative Investigations into Managed Futures Trading Programs." Managed Account Research, 2010.

Trade Everything

1. See http://www.clarkecap.com.

2. See http://www.abrahamtrading.com.

3. Francais Vaca quoted in CTA Confidential, "An Ongoing Series of Qualitative Investigations into Managed Futures Trading Programs." Managed Account Research, 2010.

Drawdown

1.   Covel, *Trend Following*, p. 263.

Entry

1.   Ed Seykota. See http://www.seykota.com.

This Way to the Egress

1.   Peter Borish speaking at TradeTech Europe 2008. Paris, April 2008.

2.   Covel, *Trend Following*, p. 264.

Losers Average Losers

1.   Jesse L. Livermore, *How to Trade in Stocks: The Livermore Formula for Combining Time Element and Price.* New York: Duel, Sloan & Pearce, 1940.

2.   Ed Seykota. See http://www.seykota.com.

Home Run

1.   Michael J. Mauboussin and Kristen Bartholdson, "The Babe Ruth Effect: Frequency versus Magnitude." *The Consilient Observer.* Vol. 1, No. 2, January 29, 2002.

2.   Michael Lewis, *Moneyball: The Art of Winning an Unfair Game.* New York: W.W. Norton and Company, 2003.

3.   Greg Burns, "Former 'Turtle' Turns Caution into an Asset." *Chicago Sun-Times*, May 29, 1989, p. 33.

Robust

1.   Dave Druz interview with Covel, 2011.

2.   Covel, *Trend Following*, p. 271.

3.   Ken Tropin speaking on "Systematic Trading Strategies in Managed Futures." The Greenwich Roundtable, November 20, 2003.

4.   Futures Industry Association Review: Interview: Money Managers. See http://www.fiafii.org.

Push the Button

1.   Television commercial introducing the new Apple McIntosh computer, January 1984.

2.   Sharon Schwartzman, "Computers Keep Funds in Mint Condition: A Major Money Manager Combines the Scientific Approach with Human Ingenuity." *Wall Street Computer Review*, Vol. 8, No. 6, March 1991, 13.

3.   Ibid.

4.   George Crapple speaking on "Systematic Trading Strategies in Managed Futures." The Greenwich Roundtable, November 20, 2003.

5.   Chuck Cain blog post, January 9, 2011. See http://www.michaelcovel.com/2011/01/09/computers-are-uselesswithout-you/.

Wash, Rinse, Repeat

1.   Gregory J. Millman, *The Chief Executive*. January–February 2003.

2.   Herb Greeenberg, "Answering the Question—Who Wins From Derivatives Losers." *The San Francisco Chronicle*, March 20, 1995, D1.

3.   Alexander M. Ineichen, *Absolute Returns*. New York: John Wiley & Sons, Inc., 2003, p. 416.

4.   Michael J. Mauboussin and Kristen Bartholdson, "Integrating the Outliers: Two Lessons from the St. Petersburg Paradox." *The Consilient Observer*. Vol. 2, No. 2, January 28, 2003.

5.   "Trend Following: Performance, Risk, and Correlation Characteristics." White Paper, Graham Capital Management. See http://www.grahamcapital.com.

Zero-Sum

1.   Larry Harris, *Trading and Exchanges: Market Microstructure for Practitioners*. New York: Oxford University Press, 2003.

2.   Larry Harris, "The Winners and Losers of the Zero-Sum Game: The Origins of Trading Profits, Price Efficiency and Market Liquidity." Draft 0.911, May 7, 1993.

3.   Ibid.

4.   Dave Druz interview with Covel, 2011.

5.   Ibid.

6.   Ibid.

7.   Ibid.

Crash and Burn

1.   George Bernard Shaw, Irish Literary.

2.   "Trend Following: Performance, Risk, and Correlation Characteristics." White Paper, Graham Capital Management. See https://www.grahamcapital.com.

3.   See http://www.wired.com/wiredscience/2011/03/market-panic-signs.

4.   See http://www.zerohedge.com/article/guest-post-beware-extrapolating-trends.

Inefficient Markets

1. Simon Kerr, "Winton Capital Management: Simon Kerr talks with David Harding." *The Hedge Fund Journal*, September 2005.

2. Roger Lowenstein, *When Genius Failed*. New York: Random House, 2000, p. 34.

3. Lowenstein, *When Genius Failed*, p. 69.

4. Broadcast Transcript, "Trillion Dollar Bet." *Nova*, No. 2075, February 8, 2000.

5. Covel, *Trend Following*, p. 157.

6. See http://www.samurai-weapons.net.

7. See http://www.economist.com/node/18233432?story_id=18233432&fsrc=rss.

8. Adam Smith, *The Name Game*. New York: Random House, 1968.

Benchmark

1. *V for Vendetta*, dir. James McTeigue, DVD, Warner Bros., March 2006.

2. Covel, *Trend Following*, p. 178.

3. Hunter S. Thompson.

Haters

1 Dennis Miller.

2. Thomas S. Y. Ho and Sang Bin Lee, *The Oxford Guide to Financial Modeling*. Oxford University Press, 2004, p. 559.

3. Julia Werdigier and Julie Creswell, "Traders Cocoa Binge Wraps Up Chocolate Market." *New York Times*, July 24, 2010. See http://dealbook.nytimes.com/2010/07/26/traders-cocoa-binge-wraps-up-chocolate-market/.

4. See http://finance.yahoo.com/blogs/breakout/macke-purple-crayon-watch-trendlines-p-crude-gold-20110329-045606-980.html.

The Root of All Evil

1. Chuck Palahniuk, *Fight Club*. New York: W.W. Norton and Company, 1996.

2. Ayn Rand, *Atlas Shrugged*. New York: Random House, 1957.

3. Charles Faulkner in *Futures*, Vol. 22, No. 12. November 1993, p. 98.

4. Milton Friedman interview on Phil Donohue, 1979.

5. Ibid.

6. Franklin Delano Roosevelt, State of the Union Address. January 11, 1944.

Panicky Sheep

1. Lewis Carroll, *Alice's Adventures in Wonderland*. 1865.

2. Charles Faulkner.

3. Jason Zweig, "Do You Sabotage Yourself?" *Business 2.0*, May 2001.

4. David Dreman, *Contrarian Investment Strategies*. New York: Simon & Schuster, 1998.

5. Jason Zweig, "Do You Sabotage Yourself?" *Business 2.0*, May 2001.

6. Steven Pearlstein, "The New Thinking About Money Is That Your Irrationality Is Predictable." *The Washington Post*, January 27, 2002, H01.

7. Harris Collingwood, "The Sink or Swim Economy." *The New York Times*, June 8, 2003.

8. See http://www.bucks.blogs.nytimes.com.

IQ vs. EQ

1. *The Hangover*, dir. Todd Phillips, DVD, Warner Bros., June 2009.

2. Jack D. Schwager, *The New Market Wizards*. New York: Harper Business, 1992.

3. See http://finance.yahoo.com/tech-ticker/forget-harvard-and-a-4-year-degree-you-can-make-more-as-a-plumber-in-the-long-run-says-prof.-kotlikoff-536046.html.

4. Michael Covel, *The Complete TurtleTrader*. New York: HarperCollins, 2008, p. 173.

5. Daniel Goleman, *Emotional Intelligence*. New York: Bantam, 1995.

6. Daniel Goleman, "What Makes a Leader?" *Harvard Business Review*, 1998.

7. Ibid.

8. James Montier, "Global Equity Strategy: If it makes you happy." Dresdner Kleinwort Wasserstein Securities Limited, June 17, 2004.

Commitment

1. Michael Rosenberg, "Beat, Play, Love." *Sports Illustrated*, October 18, 2010.

2. Jim Simons speaking at MIT, available through MIT World video.

3. Covel, *Trend Following*, p. 207.

4. Jim Rogers, *Investment Biker*. New York: Random House, 1994.

5. Roy W. Longstreet, *Viewpoints of a Commodity Trader*. Greenville: Traders Press, 1968.

6. Jack D. Schwager, *The New Market Wizards*. New York: Harper Business, 1992.

7. Covel, *Trend Following*, p. 283-284.

8. Joey Reiman, *Thinking for a Living: Creating Ideas That Revitalize Your Business, Career, and Life*. Atlanta: Longstreet Press, 2001.

9. Paul Arden, *It's Not How Good You Are, It's How Good You Want To Be: The World's Best Selling Book*. New York: Phaidon Press, 2003.

Decide Now

1. Mark Douglas, *Trading in the Zone: Master the Market with Confidence, Discipline and a Winning Attitude*. New York: New York Institute of Finance, 2001, p. 130–131.

2. Carla Fried, "The Problem with Your Investment Approach." *Business 2.0*, November 2003, p. 146.

3. Hal Lux, "The Secret World of Jim Simons." *Institutional Investor*, Vol. 34, No. 11, November 1, 2000, p. 38.

4. Gerd Gigerenzer and Peter M. Todd, *Simple Heuristics That Make Us Smart*. New York: Oxford University Press, 1999, p. 14.

5. Ibid.

6. Gerd Gigerenzer, "Smart Heuristics." Edge Foundation, Inc., March 31, 2003. See http://www.edge.org.

7. Buddha.

Science

1. Simon Kerr, "Winton Capital Management: Simon Kerr talks with David Harding." *The Hedge Fund Journal*, September 2005.

2. Chuck Cain blog post, January 9, 2011. See http://www.michaelcovel.com/2011/01/09/computers-are-uselesswithout-you/.

3. Ibid.

4. Ibid.

Statistical Thinking

1. *No Country for Old Men*, dir. Joel Coen and Ethan Coen, DVD, Miramax Films Paramount Vantage, 2007.

2. Hal Lux, "Risk Gets Riskier." *Institutional Investor*, October 2002, p. 57.

3. Jez Liberty blog entry, October 2009. See http://www.automated-trading-system.com/why-trend-following-works-look-at-the-distribution/.

4. Paul Mulvaney. Covel interview 2011.

5. See http://www.baseball-reference.com/players/p/pujolal01.shtml.

6. "Elementary Concepts in Statistics." StatSoft Electronic Statistics Textbook. See http://www.statsoft.com/textbook/elementary-concepts-in-statistics/.

7. "Systematic Global Macro: Performance, Risk, and Correlation Characteristics." Graham Capital Management, L. P., January, 2009. See http://www.grahamcapital.com.

Aha!

1. Lao Tsu, Verse XXXIII, *Tao Te Ching*.

2. See http://www.forbes.com/profile/paul-tudor-jones.

3. *Trader: The Documentary*, PBS Film, 1987.

4. Ibid.

5. Ibid.

6. Ibid.

Hero Worship

1. Orlando A. Battista, Canadian-American author.

2. *King of the Hill*, "New Cowboy on the Block." Dir. Cyndi Tang-Loveland, Episode 152, November 16, 2003.

Buy and Hope

1. James Rohrbach blog post in response to "Out of Thin Air" article, May 20, 2008. See http://www.michaelcovel.com/2008/05/20/out-of-thin-air/.

2. Ariel Nelson, "Dow and the Depression." October 10, 2008. See http://www.cnbc.com/id/27119471/Dow_and_the_Depression.

3. David Merkel blog post, April 25, 2009. See http://www.michaelcovel.com/2009/04/25/david-merkel-defending-a-wrong-view-to-the-bitter-end/.

Convert

1. Kenny Rogers, "The Gambler." Writer Don Schlitz, United Artists, 1978.

2. Martin Kronicle, "Bill Dunn: Unbreakable." *Trader Monthly*, September 2008.

Oracle of Omaha

1. Thomas Harris, *The Silence of the Lambs*. New York: St. Martin's Press, 1988.

2. Davide Dukcevich, "Buffett's Doomsday Scenario." May 6, 2002. See http://www.forbes.com/2002/05/06/0506buffett.html.

3. Ibid.

4. News Release. Berkshire Hathaway, Inc. May 22, 2002.

5. *Washington Post*, March 6, 2003, E01.

6. Cullen Roche, "The Many Myths of Warren Buffett." See http://pragcap.com/the-many-myths-of-warren-buffett.

7. See http://www.fool.com/investing/general/2011/03/28/buffett-warns-the-dollar-will-decline.aspx.

8. See http://english.themarker.com/warren-buffett-the-u-s-is-moving-toward-plutocracy-1.351236.

9. Michael Steinhardt interview with Joe Kernen. Tuesday April 5, 2011, CNBC.

A Seinfeld Moment

1. Michael Gibbons quoted in Michael Covel's "'Why' Doesn't Matter to the Technical Trader." *SFO Magazine*, April 24, 2007.

2. Jeff Zucker, former CNBC CEO. See http://www.newsweek.com/2007/08/13/forward-into-battle.html.

3. See http://www.thefinancialphilosopher.com/2011/02/understanding-markets-nature-not-naivety-or-narcissism.html.

Snow Job

1. Alvin Toffler.

2. Jim Rohrbach blog post in response to "Trend Following is not Fundamental Analysis." January 28, 2011. See http://www.michaelcovel.com/2011/01/28/trend-following-is-not-fundamental-analysis/.

Twit Me a River

1. See http://www.citywire.co.uk/global/can-you-make-money-from-twitter/a479038?.

2. David Silverman, "The Madness of Chat Room Crowds." *SFO Magazine*, October 3, 2005.

Goldline

1. Jay Z, "Big Pimpin," Vol. 3... Life and Times of S. Carter, Roc-A-Fella and Def Jam, April 11, 2000.

2. Victor Niederhoffer.

Intoxication

1. *Larry King Live*. CNN, March 30, 2001.

2. Robert Schmidt, "Geithner Slams Bonuses, Says Banks Would Have Failed (Update2)." *Bloomberg*, December 4, 2009.

3. Ben Bernanke on CBS's *60 Minutes*, December 5, 2010.

4. Ben Bernanke, Interview on CNBC's *Squawk Box*. July 1, 2005.

5. Ben Bernanke, House of Representatives hearing, February 15, 2006. See http://www.federalreserve.gov/newsevents/testimony/bernanke20060215a.htm.

6. Ben Bernanke, "The Economic Outlook." Testimony before the Joint Economic Committee, Congress, March 28, 2007. See http://www.federalreserve.gov/newsevents/testimony/bernanke20070328a.htm.

7. Niall Ferguson speaking at the Aspen Ideas Festival, Aspen, Colorado, July 8, 2010.

8. Federal Open Market Committee (FOMC), "Transcripts and Other Historical Materials." June 2005. To download a full PDF, see http://pragcap.com/the-fed-knew-about-the-impending-housing-bust.

9. See http://www.cfr.org/content/publications/attachments/infi_1277_Rev6.pdf.

10. Jeremy Grantham, "Pavlov's Bulls." GMO Quarterly Newsletter, January 2011.

11. Robert B. Cialdini, *Influence: The Psychology of Persuasion*. New York: William Morrow and Co., 1993, p. 168.

12. Nassim Nicholas Taleb, *The Bed of Procrustes*. New York: Random House, 2010, p. 31.

13. Tyler Durden, "Vix Closes at Lowest Level Since Summer of 2007." January 14, 2011. See http://www.zerohedge.com/article/vix-closes-lowest-level-summer-2007.

Parliament of Whores

1. *The Matrix*, dir. Andy and Larry Wachowski, DVD, Warner Bros. Pictures, 1999.

2. Cullen Roche, "David Rosenberg Attacks the Fed's Intentional Ponzi Approach." October 5, 2010. See http://pragcap.com/david-rosenberg-attacks-the-feds-intentional-ponzi-approach.

3. Ariana Eunjung Cha, "China Leaves Small Investors Behind on Road to Capitalism." *Washington Post Foreign Service*, May 3, 2008. See http://www.washingtonpost.com/wp-dyn/content/article/2008/05/02/AR2008050204009.html.

Crowded House

1. Zen proverb.

2. Keith Campbell, Campbell & Co., Managed Account Reports.

Black Box

1. *South Park*, "Chief Aid," episode 27, October 7, 1998.

2. "Black box." See http://en.wikipedia.org/wiki/Black_box.

3. Ben Hogan.

4. Shaun Jordan video interview, "Managed Futures with Abraham Trading Co." March 8, 2011. See http://www.cmegroup.com/education/managed-futures-with-abraham-trading-co.html.

5. Blog entry. See http://www.michaelcovel.com.

6. Blog response to "The reason people gave Madoff money; same reason they don't give it to Trend Followers." January 5, 2011. See http://www.michaelcovel.com.

Lucky Monkey

1. The Pixies, "Monkey Gone to Heaven." *Doolittle*, Elektra, 1989.

2. Frederic Tomesco, "Obama's Stimulus Plan Made Crisis Worse Taleb Says." *Bloomberg Businessweek*, September 25, 2010.

3. Bill Simmons, "You Can Quote Me on This." October 11, 2002. See http://sports.espn.go.com/espn/page2/story?page=simmons/vault/021011.

Honest

1. Lao Tzu.

2. Michael Shermer, *The Skeptic: Encyclopedia of Pseudoscience*. Santa Barbara: ABC-Cleo Inc., 2002.

3. See http://www.cnbc.com/id/42297221.

4. Tim Ferriss, "The Benefits of Pissing People Off." November 25, 2009. See http://www.fourhourworkweek.com.

5. Ibid.

6. David Turnbull. See http://davidturnbull.com/2009/11/05/a-love-for-criticism.

7. Ibid.

8. Ibid.

9. Ibid.

10. Public Enemy, "911 is a Joke." *Fear of a Black Planet*, Def Jam Records, March 22, 1990.

Under the Radar

1. Laurie Kaplan, "Turning Turtles into Traders." *Managed Derivatives*, May 1996.

2. John Waggoner, "How rational is stock market?" *USA Today*, May 14, 2011. See http://www.usatoday.com/MONEY/usaedition/2011-02-15-efficientmarket15_CV_U.htm.

Ethos

1. Florence and the Machine, "The Dog Days Are Over." Lungs, Universal Island, December 1, 2008.

2. See http://www.sethgodin.typepad.com.

3. See http://www.michaelcovel.com/2009/11/08/michael-covel-business-philosophy/.

4. See http://sportsillustrated.cnn.com/2011/writers/michael_rosenberg/03/27/vcu.butler/index.html.

5. See http://www.michaelcovel.com/2009/11/08/michael-covel-business-philosophy/.

6. *The Hangover*, dir. Todd Philips, per. Zach Galifianakis, DVD, Warner Bros, 2009.

Games People Play

1. John Lennon, "Nobody Told Me." *Milk and Honey*, Polydor Records, 1984.

2. Alexander M. Ineichen, *Absolute Returns.* New York: John Wiley & Sons, 2003, p. 64.

3. Lara Logan interviews Bill Walters on CBS's *60 Minutes*, January 16, 2011.

Blood Hound

1. *Patton*, dir. Franklin J. Schaffner, perf. George C. Scott, 20th Century Fox, 1970.

2. David Shenk, *The Genius in All of Us: Why Everything You've Been Told About Genetics Talent, and IQ Is Wrong.* New York: Random House, 2010, p. 11.

3. See http://www.michaelcovel.com/2010/02/06/meeting-mikhail-gorbachev-my-journey/.

4. Anthony Robbins, *Unlimited Power: The New Science of Personal Achievement.* New York: Free Press, 1986, p. 12.

5. John Tierney, "When Every Child Is Good Enough." *New York Times*, November 21, 2004. See http://www.nytimes.com/2004/11/21/weekinreview/21tier.html.

6. Mark Cuban, "Success and Motivation—You Only Have to Be Right Once." May 30, 2005. See http://blogmaverick.com/2005/05/30/success-and-motivation-you-only-have-to-be-right-once/.

Epilogue

1. Lynyrd Skynyrd, "Free Bird." MCA Records, 1974.

2. VCU NCAA Final Four chant.

3. Nassim Nicholas Taleb, *The Bed of Procrustes.* New York: Random House, 2010, p. 39.

Surprise, Surprise, Surprise

1. See http://reason.com/archives/2011/04/05/future-babble.

2. See http://video.cnbc.com/gallery/?video=3000015574.

3. Ibid.

4. Ibid.

5. Ibid.

6. Ibid.

7. Kris Devasabai, "Managed Futures on the Rise as Investors Chase Diversification." *Hedge Funds Review*, April 4, 2011. See http://www.hedgefundsreview.com/hedge-funds-review/feature/2035509/managed-futures-rise-investors-chase-diversification.

8. See http://video.cnbc.com/gallery/?video=3000015574.

9. Ibid.

10. Ibid.

11. Ibid.

12. Ibid.

13. See http://www.criticalthinking.org/aboutCT/define_critical_thinking.cfm.

Origins

1. James Grant, *The Great Metropolis*, second series volume II (London, 1837), p. 81.

2. Arthur W. Cutten, "The Story of a Speculator." *Saturday Evening Post* (December 3, 1932), p.13.

3. Edwin Lefèvre, *Reminiscences of a Stock Operator*. Garden City, New York: The Sun Dial Press, 1923, p. 54.

4. Ibid., p. 54.

5. Ibid., p. 115.

6. Henry Clews, *Twenty-eight Years in Wall Street*. New York: Irving Publishing, 1888, p. 20.

7. Robert R. Prechter, Jr., *R. N. Elliott's Masterworks: The Definitive Collection*. Gainsville: New Classics Library, 1994, p. 50.

8. Robert D. Edwards and John Magee, *Technical Analysis of Stock Trends*, 5th edition. Boston: 1966, p. 234.

9. William D. Gann, *Truth of the Stock Tape*. New York: 1930, p. 33.

10. Richard D. Wyckoff, *Studies in Tape Reading*. New York: Financial Guardian Publishing Company, 1924, p. 7.

11. Richard D. Wyckoff, *Stock Market Technique Number 2*. Fraser Publishing Company, 1989, reprint of 1934 edition, p. 197.

12. Wyckoff, *Studies in Tape Reading*. p. 131.

13. Lefèvre, *Reminiscences of a Stock Operator*. p. 101.

14. Ibid., p. 213.

15. Jesse L. Livermore, *How to Trade in Stocks: The Livermore Formula for Combining Time Element and Price.* New York: Duel, Sloan & Pearce, 1940, p. 20.

16. Ibid., p. 24.

17. Alfred E. Cowles III and Herbert E. Jones, "Some a Posteriori Probabilities in Stock Market Actions." *Econometrica,* July 1937, p. 286.

18. Alfred Winslow Jones, "Fashions in Forecasting." *Fortune,* March 1949, p. 180.

19. William Dunnigan, *New Blueprints for Gains in Stocks and One-way Formula for Trading in Stocks and Commodities.* United Kingdom: Harriman House Limited, 2005, reprint of 1954 and 1956 editions, p. 31.

20. Ibid., p. 32.

21. Elmer Clark Bratt, *Business Cycles and Forecasting,* fourth edition. Homewood, Illinois: Richard D. Irwin Inc., 1953, p. 497.

22. Richard D. Donchian, "Trend-Following Methods in Commodity Price Analysis." *Commodity Year Book,* 1957, p. 35.

23. William Baldwin, "Rugs to Riches." *Forbes,* March 1, 1982, p. 143.

24. Darrell Jobman, "Richard Donchian: Pioneer of Trend-Trading." *Commodities,* September 1980, p. 42.

25. Soren Kierkegaard.

Cheat Sheet

1. Seth Godin, *Poke the Box.* The Domino Project, 2011.

2. Ben Hogan.

Quick Commandments

1. T. S. Eliot.

2. Bernard Malamud, *The Natural.* New York: Harcourt Brace, 1952.

About Trend Following & Michael Covel

1. *The Dark Knight,* dir. Christopher Nolan, perf. Heath Ledger, DVD, Legendary Pictures Syncopy Films, July 14, 2008.

*If you're good at something,
never do it for free.*[1]

About Trend Following & Michael Covel

Michael W. Covel serves as President of Trend Following (TurtleTrader®), a privately owned research firm. In 1996, Covel colaunched TurtleTrader.com®. It has attracted millions of visitors.

His first book is *Trend Following: How Great Traders Make Millions in Up or Down Markets* (FT Press, Apr. 04, Nov. 05, Feb. 07, and Feb. 09). This must-have classic has been translated in German, Japanese, Chinese (Traditional and Simplified), Korean, French, Arabic, Turkish, Portuguese, and Russian.

His second book, *The Complete TurtleTrader: The Legend, the Lessons, the Results* (Collins, Oct. 07 and Feb. 09), is the only narrative account of trader Richard Dennis and his student traders, the Turtles. It has become the definitive book on the subject and has been translated in German, Japanese, Chinese (Traditional and Simplified), Korean, and Russian.

His first documentary film is *Broke: The New American Dream*. It explores human behavior and trend following during the 2007-2009 market crash and premiered on *The Documentary Channel*® fall 2009. The film was shot in 13 major cities on three continents. Top traders Larry Hite, Jim Rogers, David Harding, Mark Mobius, and Bill Miller appear. Nobel Prize winners Harry Markowitz and Vernon Smith also appear.

Blog

www.covel.com

Trend Following Research Services

www.trendfollowing.com

- Trading Systems
- System Code
- Newsletters
- Consulting
- Seminars
- Film: www.brokemovie.com

Original TurtleTrader®

www.turtletrader.com

Michael Covel Twitter

www.twitter.com/covel

Michael Covel Facebook

www.facebook.com/covel

Trend Commandments **Book**

www.trendcommandments.com

Free Resources

- Video intro: www.trendfollowing.com/free.html
- Newsletter: www.trendfollowing.com/list.html
- Resources: www.trendfollowing.com/resources.html

Email

info@trendfollowing.com

info@trendcommandments.com

Note: How does Michael Covel pronounce his last name? Co-vell. "Co" rhymes with toe. "Vell" rhymes with bell. Equally accented each syllable. It was shortened from Covalesky, which was shortened originally from Kavaliauskas.

Index

FINANCIAL TIMES

In an increasingly competitive world, it is quality
of thinking that gives an edge—an idea that opens new
doors, a technique that solves a problem, or an insight
that simply helps make sense of it all.

We work with leading authors in the various arenas
of business and finance to bring cutting-edge thinking
and best-learning practices to a global market.

It is our goal to create world-class print publications
and electronic products that give readers
knowledge and understanding that can then be
applied, whether studying or at work.

To find out more about our business
products, you can visit us at www.ftpress.com.